WHAT EFFECTIVE
LEADERS DO

A BUSINESS PARABLE ABOUT DEVELOPING
AWARENESS, CHALLENGING ASSUMPTIONS,
REFINING FOCUS, AND GROWING CONFIDENCE

SEAN GLAZE

The successful teamwork, culture,
and productivity EVERY organization seeks
are ALL symptoms of LEADERSHIP.

Businesses rise or fall based on the
quality of LEADERS – and EVERY leader
can become <u>MORE EFFECTIVE</u>.

EFFECTIVE
— LEADERS —

CONTACT SEAN!

Book Sean as a Speaker to **Accelerate the Growth of Your Team** at Your Next Corporate Event or Conference

Visit Him Online at:
https://stickycultures.com/

sticky cultures

or
http://greatresultsteambuilding.com

ISBNs
Paperback: 979-8-9856769-3-8
Hardback: 979-8-9856769-6-9
eBook: 979-8-9856769-4-5

DEDICATION

*To the winning teammates promoted beyond
their expertise to a position of greater impact...
To the leaders committed to staying coachable
and improving their team's performance.
And to the people interested in accelerating
the growth and success of those they care about.
This story was written for YOU!*

TABLE OF CONTENTS

EFFECTIVE
— LEADERS —

PREFACE

WHY READ THIS BOOK?

As a basketball coach, I eventually learned that the most effective tool to accelerate PLAYER DEVELOPMENT was investing in my development as their coach. That holds true in business as well. The most effective tool to ensure the development of YOUR TEAM is the investment in your development as a LEADER.

When I speak at a conference, or on a call coaching leaders from around the country, I consistently meet very talented people who have done a phenomenal job in their role... Then they got promoted to a leadership position that requires skills and insights beyond their previous area of expertise. And those good people—smart and capable people like you—start looking for ways to accelerate their growth as leaders, so they can be MORE EFFECTIVE.

There is the challenge for most leaders.

They are willing and, at the same time, quite unaware of

HOW to drastically improve their perspective, increase their confidence, and boost their impact.

So, how do you become <u>truly effective</u> as a leader?

You've probably heard of intentional leadership, courageous leadership, remarkable leadership, inclusive leadership, compassionate leadership, authentic leadership—

But you can be intentional, courageous, and authentic... read all the books... and still not truly be effective in creating the exceptional culture and results you want.

EFFECTIVENESS is the ultimate destination other meandering paths hope to eventually lead you to...

You have likely realized that everything becomes easy once you understand how to do it... Just like tying your shoes or riding a bicycle.

And the same is true in leadership!

Remember slapping your forehead at some point in your past because you were embarrassed to admit you didn't realize how obvious or simple the thing was that you had been frustrated by a moment before?

Those "forehead moments" that we ALL experience are a result of admitting that what was once difficult for you really seems simple now you understand it. And YOUR success as a leader—getting your people to deliver better results instead of better excuses—is about becoming more effective.

The successful team building, GREAT culture, and more productive teamwork you desire is ALL a symptom of better, more effective leadership.

Thankfully, being more EFFECTIVE is not about being smarter... You are already smart enough. You just need to <u>increase your awareness and adopt more productive beliefs, which will produce more fruitful behaviors.</u>

Answering that question, "*How do you become more effective as a leader?*" has been my passion and purpose since my first season as a high school basketball coach over three decades ago...

Unfortunately for the players, I was painfully ineffective early on, and I was responsible for many losses in my career as I grew and learned. But those early losses inspired my journey to seek insights, tools, and techniques to help me become better.

And that desire to learn and grow was crucial... Because if I had been complacent instead of coachable, our team performance would likely not have improved.

That is likely why you have found this book—YOU realize that for your team to be better, you must become more effective.

Because the quality of YOUR leadership is the determining factor in your team's performance. And, if you remained in your current position without improving your effectiveness, you realize that adding years of experience would not significantly impact your results.

Experience alone does not develop more effective leaders. On your journey through your career, it is what you NOTICE during your experiences that increases your awareness... And, as you will soon learn as part of the story that follows, greater AWARENESS is what allows you to become more effective.

Of course, every book is a journey. There may be different characters, conflicts, and circumstances... But the ultimate desired result of reading a book is an entertaining experience that inspires a change in you, the reader. Without a change in perspective and an introduction of new behaviors, the hours spent reading would be considered empty.

So... I wrote this book with TWO goals in mind:

1. **TO ENTERTAIN YOU**, SO YOU KEEP READING FOR 2–3 HOURS AND HIGHLIGHT SOME KEY IDEAS FROM THE BOOK.
2. **TO EQUIP YOU**, SO YOU START APPLYING A FEW VALUABLE INSIGHTS AND BECOME A MORE EFFECTIVE LEADER.

If I can accomplish both goals, the book will have done its job!

I hope you will take just a moment to review the book on Amazon or recommend it to a friend or two who might benefit from its story and insights as well ;)

Thanks in advance for trusting me with your time—

Let's get started!

EFFECTIVE
— LEADERS —

CHAPTER 1

COMPLAINTS

Jenn woke up feeling groggy... She instinctively reached over to discover the other side of the bed was empty. Without Brian there, she had taken Nyquil to help her sleep, because she always seemed to just toss and turn when she was alone. The medicine had worked too well.

She rested there on her back for a moment, then rubbed her eyes with the thumb and pointer of her left hand, and reached over to the bedside table with her right, grabbing her phone to check the time.

Surprise and panic jolted her upright - it was after 8:00. No time for coffee before her video call with Maria. She had to put on a blouse, wash her face, and sign onto the call. All in the next 11 minutes...

After the tornado of her rushed morning routine - including brushing teeth, pulling her brown mess of hair back into a ponytail, and finding an appropriate top in her closet - she left the bedroom and headed down the hall.

Taking a deep breath, fixing a loose strand of hair behind her ear, Jenn collected herself as she entered the bedroom they had turned into her home office workspace.

She bumped her knee clumsily into one of the cardboard boxes still waiting to be unpacked, and mumbled a quick "dang-it" to herself. Then she finally made it to her computer desk and collapsed into the chair, leaning back and sighing heavily, overcome with a craving for the coffee her body was accustomed to.

She signed into her Teams account and turned on the ring light above her laptop...

Maria hadn't joined the meeting yet.

Dooley pranced into the room as Jenn waited for the call to begin... That made her smile.

Dooley was her cockapoo, a lovable twelve-pound bundle of snuggly tan fluff and sweetness that had been hers since before she met Brian. His routine was usually to wait for her downstairs on the couch and watch her finish her first cup of coffee before walking him. Maybe he needed to go out?

He nudged her leg with his nose to say hello, then lifted his front paws onto her thigh, looking for attention.

His front paws were wet. Had he been splashing in his water bowl?

His tail wagged excitedly as she scratched behind his ears. *"Gimme fifteen minutes, sweet boy! I've gotta talk to somebody from work first, okay?"*

Jenn turned her focus back to the laptop screen, and wondered where Maria was.

Dooley pounced on his chew toy and then dragged it under the desk to his poofy dog bed, where he spent most of each day while she worked.

It was now 8:35. Maria was late. Jenn opened another browser tab to check her email. In her sent folder was her invitation to Maria for the meeting.

She saw in the corner of her screen that the time was now 8:40... "Dammit," she thought, disappointed with Maria. She wanted to talk with her before the call with Lewis.

She opened up a new email draft and thought about what she would send to Maria.

A few moments later, she started typing.

> "Hi Maria—
>
> We need to talk...
>
> You can't just not show up to a meeting.
>
> Need those reports by Thursday!
>
> Jenn"

She breathed out through her nose and hit send. This is not what she needed today.

She closed the video conferencing and email tabs, and got up out of the chair. *"Come on, Dooley-bear! Ready for your walk?"*

He didn't budge from his bed. He was busy gnawing on his rubber chicken. That made Jenn smile again.

And before she left the room, at precisely 9:00 am EST, her phone rang. The name Lewis Patton popped up on her Teams meeting screen. It was her boss. The owner of the company she worked for.

She grabbed the folders of information she expected he would want to review with her: all the updated data on her team's current projects.

"Hello Lewis." She adjusted herself in the chair a bit.

"Good morning, Jenn. How are you?" He looked directly into his camera as he asked. A serious face. Behind his bald head, Jen could see pictures and books on his wall of shelves. The fluorescent light in his office made his face pale and shadowy.

"Good, I guess. Just had somebody no-show a call, but I'll take care of it. Everything is moving along. Should be ready to share the detail drawings for the Bakersfield Project by end of week."

Jenn thought about Chris, Brandon, and Tanya as she said it, proud of the work they did as her most dependable team members.

"That's good to hear... Any updates on the Columbus or Houston jobs?" His eyes were now down, listening for her reply. He was looking at papers on his desk.

"Yeah..." She found the two folders to be able to discuss them. *"They are both, uh, a little behind. But I think the, uh..."*

Lewis looked back up, directly at the camera, sighed, and interrupted her. *"Jenn, you know what... let's talk bigger picture here. That's why I called you today. Not just about your current projects, but to discuss how things have been going for you with managing your team."* He paused a moment.

Jenn put the folders down on her keyboard and tilted her head, waiting for Lewis to continue.

"I know the transition hasn't been easy... but we're about sixty days in, and the truth is I'm afraid you weren't very prepared to move into this role..."

Jenn's eyes grew wide and her heart sank.

"Listen, I saw a stat that like 60% of new managers fail—it's not an easy job. And it is so much different from what you did for us in your other role..." He paused a beat to let her process the words.

Then he frowned as he began to speak again, and the ceiling office lights cast shadows on his face that made him look morbid. *"You are a great design engineer. But managing a team is... different. And your team has had so many issues the last month or so... it's just affecting our project timelines. I don't doubt how smart and capable you are, Jenn. But I'm afraid I've done a poor job of supporting you. Do you feel up to it?"*

She waited quietly for a moment. How was she supposed to respond to that? The job WAS different. Of course she knew THAT. But that was also what had excited her about the opportunity. Something new. A challenge. And the big bump in pay certainly didn't hurt with them buying a house and now having a mortgage. Especially helpful with

Brian taking a pay cut. They needed her income now. She couldn't make the budget work if she lost this position.

She shook her head and gathered herself. *"Lewis... You are not wrong about the issues we've had. But I think we're getting it under control now, and the team is getting ready to turn the corner you wanted when you gave me the job in the first place..."*

Lewis looked up, directly at his camera. *"Jenn... it's just that, you've already had one person leave, and if productivity is suffering, we need to do something. We can't have your people not be on the same page... and you just had one of them not show up to a call?"*

Jenn shook her head for emphasis of her next comment. She couldn't lose this job! *"That's not fair, Lewis. I've got this. There's always issues with a transition. You have to trust me. I've GOT this!"*

Lewis frowned. He rubbed his mouth and chin for a moment. And finally, he nodded slightly and spoke. *"Okay, Jenn. I want to believe you. You were my choice. You know that. But we can't have any more costly delays or people leaving. The large projects your people are responsible for designing right now—they are very important to our company."*

"Absolutely."

"Okay..." Lewis moved his hand across the screen. *"No more talk about that then. Those folders you had in your hand... anything inside them that would keep us from hitting the initial milestone projections?"*

"No sir." Had she dodged the bullet?

"Great. Anything you need from me, you let me know. I want this to work... for both of us, Jenn. Just want you to be able to handle the team."

"Absolutely. I understand..."

"Great. Let's touch base again in a week to see how things are going. I'll send you a calendar invitation, and keep me informed of anything that would affect our timelines for those projects."

"Yes sir. On it."

"Okay, Jenn. Have a good day."

"You too..."

"Yep... Goodbye."

She clicked to close the window on her laptop screen. That conversation was over. She had not expected it to go like that, though.

Things had not been perfect, of course. With Susan leaving unexpectedly, and some other team members not communicating their progress with her or being late with assignments. But that was not all on her, right? Every team has issues. Especially in a hybrid situation, with her unable to peek into their offices for check-ins. It's one thing to lead a team on site. But being apart all but one day a week felt like herding cats sometimes.

If she wanted to keep her job, though, she knew she needed to be better. She needed to address some of their behaviors. Being angry at them wasn't the answer. Barking at them wasn't going to improve their talks with her, and probably wouldn't gain the respect she wanted. She thought that maybe she really wasn't the right person for the job.

Then she thought about Brian. She wished he was here. Being separated from your spouse was tough.

She looked at Dooley curled up in his bed under her desk. And she thought for a moment about how interesting it was, how the person you choose to share your life with affects the quality of it?

Just a few years ago, in a very different relationship, her last boyfriend made her feel small. She had suffered through nearly a year of thinking he was right... that she was incompetent and lucky to not be alone. She didn't remember many good days from that year... And she was proud of herself for breaking that off.

Then she got excited when she met Brian at the gym, and discovered something so much healthier in their relationship.

They married six months later.

He was working as an assistant college basketball coach. He was thoughtful and made her feel special. He always found a way to make her smile. And his cute dimple and the fact that he was in great shape didn't hurt...

But now he was away for twelve days overseas with the team. Their season would start soon, and the players and coaches were practicing and playing games against club teams in Spain to prepare for their season. It was a fantastic travel experience for him.

But with her new role as head of design and engineering, Jenn had to stay home.

And Brian's team wouldn't be back until the end of August. She missed his presence... Missed having him there to talk to.

Moving into this new house... spending time together before he had left... had been so comfortable. Now she had to deal with this work stuff without him.

Her management role at **ModernSpace Workstations** was more challenging than she had expected. Not having him there to discuss her problems or just encourage her with his adorable grin made her feel even more alone. And her feeling of isolation extended to the team. She felt distant from them.

She didn't know how to fix the things that were affecting the performance she had promised Lewis she would improve. Yes, some behaviors on the team were concerning... So, it seemed her honeymoon as a leader was over.

Her husband had said many times that the danger with coaching was that 'if you're on the losing side of the scoreboard, people will look for someone to blame it on...'

That was why Lewis had said what he said. But this was the first time she had been on the wrong side of any scoreboard at work.

She was a hard worker. She was dependable and smart. That's why they asked her to take on the management position after Phil left... And Jenn liked a challenge.

She was excited that they tapped her for the role. She was smart, capable, and coachable. But the last few weeks had been frustrating. The people she was responsible for managing were far less predictable than the numbers and drawings she had grown skilled at manipulating.

She was great with all the technical stuff in her previous role. But leadership was not a skill she had developed—and there was no handbook she knew of for how to navigate these new challenges.

Jenn shook her head to clear her thoughts and looked lovingly down at Dooley. *"Okay, sweetness. Let's get momma a big cup of coffee, and then get you out on your walk. Sound good?"*

Dooley's hindquarters shook with excitement, and he danced under her feet with anticipation as they started down the steps.

She wanted so badly to call Brian and tell him about her conversation with Lewis. But part of her was afraid to bother him with her struggles. He was dealing with his own issues, building trust with a new coaching staff. And she wasn't even sure what time it was over there, so she didn't want to interrupt him from sleep or practice or whatever he might be in the middle of...

She needed that coffee.

But as she descended the steps, she started checking social media for anything interesting... And without a thought, she stepped down onto the first-floor carpeting, and a short walk to the kitchen and the Keurig dark roast that she had been craving.

But she stopped and her mouth dropped in shock when her right foot hit the carpet. Her eyes went immediately from her phone screen to the floor, as her socked feet pressed into the fibers and delivered an unexpectedly damp sensation.

The carpet was soaking wet. And now her right sock was, too. Carpet isn't supposed to squish! But as Jenn stood with her left foot on the bottom step and looked down, she could see that the entire first floor of the house was covered in an inch or so of water.

She HAD to call Brian.

Her thumb instinctively found him in her "recents" list, and she now understood why Dooley's paws had been wet. Her body shook as dread and confusion ran through her, waiting for him to pick up. But there was no answer. It went to his voicemail. He was 4,000 miles away, and she didn't know what to do…

Dooley was still on the next to last step and hopped up, twisting his body against her left calf as he impatiently celebrated the anticipation of his morning walk.

Jenn called Brian again, but it went to voicemail again.

And then a few moments later, her phone vibrated. It was Lewis.

Her thumb tapped the screen to answer it… *"Hello?"*

"Hi Jenn—I've been thinking more about our earlier conversation. I'm still…"

Jenn broke in to interrupt him. *"My house is flooded, Lewis. There's water all over the floor! And I can't get Brian on the phone..."* She heard more panic in her voice than she wanted. But she wasn't sure what to do next.

After a moment's silence, Lewis replied. *"It's okay, Jenn. You can handle it. Just need to call a plumber..."* He paused, then his voice changed to one of almost excitement. *"You know what—I know somebody that can help you. Lookup Estrada Plumbing. It's a good company that you can trust. They'll take care of you."*

"Thanks, Lewis. Okay. I'll do that... And uh... why were you calling back?"

"I was just going to say that, while I'm still concerned about the issues we discussed, I want to believe in you. Let's push our follow-up chat to after my vacation. I'm back the first of September, and that'll give you time to deal with all this. We'll talk at the office that Tuesday, okay?"

The first of September was two weeks away. But her house was flooding NOW. She had to deal with this.

"Okay, Lewis... Thanks. Talk then. I'm gonna call that plumber." And she hung up.

She felt the sock on her right foot heavy with water even as she lifted it. She clicked the Google Maps App on her phone and searched for Estrada Plumbing, finding they were located just eleven miles away at the top of the search list.

Estrada Plumbing had 83 five-star reviews.

Jenn touched the phone icon to call for their help. It rang five times before clicking a few times, and then a voice answered. *"Good morning, Estrada Plumbing!"*

"Hello? Hi... my name is Jenn. I need someone... my carpet is flooded... and I have no idea where it is coming from!"

"Yes ma'am, we can help with that! What is your address?" The woman had a Hispanic accent.

Jenn gave her all the information. When she hung up, she tried her husband again. Still no answer from him. Where was he? Was he okay?

Dooley sat on the last step watching her. Her thoughts were jumbled and anxious... What a morning. And still no coffee yet. That would have to wait.

She splattered through the watery floor on the way to the kitchen, grabbed Dooley's leash, and opened the door to walk him out into their back yard.

They didn't have a fence yet. Both of her feet were in thick wet socks as she watched Dooley do his business. He finished, looked up for her approval, and pranced back into the house. She gave him a treat from the jar on the counter, and loaded the coffeemaker with the Peet's dark roast cartridge and her empty mug.

The water on the kitchen floor was not very deep, but every time she stepped, her feet made a "squish" sound as her wet sock hit the tile floor. She sat at the kitchen island on a stool, keeping her feet above the floor on the low support bar of the chair, and sipped on the steamy coffee: the one thing that wasn't a disaster so far.

On her third sip, there was a knock at the front door. Through the side window, she saw a white van with a plumbing logo on the side sitting in her driveway. Her feet splashed a bit as she walked to answer the door.

On her front porch was an older man in jeans and a collared black short-sleeve knit polo shirt with the company logo. It was a red wrench and white faucet above blue lettering that said ESTRADA PLUMBING, just like on the van.

He smiled as Jenn pulled open the front door for him. *"So, ma'am, what seems to be the problem?"*

EFFECTIVE
— L E A D E R S —

CHAPTER 2

THE LADDER OF AWARENESS

The man standing in her doorway did not look like a plumber. He was in his early sixties, with a mixed gray and black stubble beard wrapped around a warm smile. Soft brown eyes were framed by substantial crow's feet of experience, and he shifted his weight a bit as he greeted her in the doorway. *"Hello, I'm Tony. You called our office?"* His voice was calm, kind, and reassuring.

Jen held the door open with her left hand and had the iPhone by her side in her right. She was frozen briefly with a look of exasperation.

She surveyed his appearance again to confirm he was truly a plumber. He was a thin, slight Hispanic man, barely as tall as she was. And he had no tool box in his hand. *"Hi Tony. I have no idea. It's just everywhere..."* She pointed at the hardwood in the foyer, which was covered by a thin layer of water, and then motioned her finger toward the kitchen.

She closed the front door, turning for him to follow her. As her socks splashed, her iPhone vibrated and then went up to her right ear— *"Brian! Let me call you back. The plumber guy just got here."*

She led Tony to the kitchen, then lifted herself back onto the stool where her mug still waited on the island, half full.

Dooley was lying beside it, curiously watching their house guest. He had a receding line of short black hair and weathered brown skin, with a high forehead that somehow emphasized the soft eyes below it. *"Any idea where the leak is?"*

His voice had very little accent. She shook her head and sighed. *"I looked around, but didn't notice anything. No idea where it is coming from. Just this soaking wet floor. And my husband is out of town..."*

Tony nodded. As he turned to survey the damage, she saw a silver wrench peeking out of his back left jeans pocket. *"Okay, ma'am. We can clean it up a bit first. I already turned off the water out front to keep it from getting any worse. We'll get you figured out soon enough..."*

"Oh... um, yes. That makes sense..." she said.

She ran upstairs, returning with a handful of towels that she used to get as much water up as possible in the kitchen and foyer.

Tony moved a few pieces of furniture onto the tile in their kitchen, then pulled up the pieces of wet carpet and padding in the hallway at the bottom of the steps and in the living room, exposing the concrete slab underneath. He dragged the carpet out to the driveway, then placed all the furniture on blocks he brought in from his van.

It took a while to dry the floor with towels, but before long there was no more flooding in her house. Jenn took off her socks and carried them up to the washroom, along with a mass of wet towels that had been wrung out and left draining in the sink.

When she came back down, Tony was pulling their refrigerator away from the wall of built-in cabinets. Jenn grabbed Dooley from the counter and held him with her right forearm, petting him with her left hand while she watched the plumber work. *"Can't believe this happened today!"*

"With your husband gone?" Tony asked.

"Not just that... I had a horrible call with my boss just before I found it. I was already worrying about my job and the problems I'm having as a new leader... and then I walk downstairs and my house is flooded... and I have no idea what is causing it or how bad the repairs are gonna be..." Jenn breathed in deep through her nose and sighed powerfully.

Tony, now kneeling behind the refrigerator, offered her a comforting smile. *"Well, I'm glad to be able to help. And I found the water problem... There's your leak!"* He pointed to a thin copper pipe behind the fridge that connected to the wall, and curled around as it rose to connect with the freezer. Tony pointed to a crimp in the thin copper pipe – and Jenn could see where it was broken open at the bend. As he held it, one tiny drop escaped and fell to the white-tiled kitchen floor.

"THAT is what did all this?" Jenn asked, eyebrows raised.

Tony nodded. *"Yes, ma'am. You'd be surprised how often it happens. Did someone move the refrigerator in the last couple of days?"*

Jenn remembered asking Brian to move it further back before he left two days earlier. She shook her head, realizing what had happened. *"I thought it was sticking out too far... Thought he could push it back a bit. Make it even with the cabinet... you know?"*

Tony used his wrench to remove the leaking pipe from the connector near the base of the wall, then stood up. He returned the wrench to his jeans back pocket. Then carried the broken pipe over to Jenn and placed it on the island's brown granite counter top. *"Well, that there is your culprit. Good thing it wasn't a busted pipe in your wall or in your concrete foundation. Still, doesn't take long to do a lot of damage."*

Jenn looked at the coil of copper on her counter and resumed petting Dooley, more to comfort herself than the dog.

"I've got some new freezer line in the van I can replace it with. Think your tile should be okay... might only need to replace the carpet."

He walked outside, and Jenn took out her phone to call Brian back.

She put Dooley back down on the floor, and he followed her dutifully as she strode back upstairs to grab a new pair of socks.

Brian answered her call on the first ring.

————

Jenn was grateful and excited to hear Brian's voice. It had barely been more than a day since he left, but she missed him terribly.

After describing the events of the morning to her husband, answering his questions and enjoying both his compassion and encouragement, he asked to talk with the plumber for a few minutes...

She had carried the phone to Tony, who was very thorough in his explanation of the situation and necessary next steps. When she got the phone back, Brian talked her through what to do next.

Jenn wrote down the list of things that needed to be done, and then shared a few loving reminders of how much she missed him before they hung up.

She would call their insurance company and worry about new carpet later. Even with a wrecked house, her mind drifted back to her team. If she wanted to be able to stay in this house more than a few more months, she needed to figure out what to do differently.

She had been a really good design engineer for **ModernSpace Workstations**. But that required a very different skill set than managing other people.

Tony finished working on the refrigerator and slid it back gently into its place, careful not to crimp the new copper line he had just installed.

Jenn was at the coffee maker for her second cup. *"Would you like to have a coffee before leaving?"*

Tony nodded politely. *"That would be nice. Thank you. Let me prepare your invoice, and I can enjoy it when I come back inside?"*

Jenn nodded and grabbed a mug from the shelf for him as he left.

When he returned, he had a clipboard and sat next to her at the kitchen island, where she had already placed his steaming mug of coffee. *"Do you need creamer? We've got vanilla if you like that?"*

"Just black, thanks."

He took a sip and smiled warmly with appreciation, then placed the mug down and slid the clipboard and invoice over to Jenn for her to inspect. *"Dark roast?"*

"Yes, it is! That's all I drink now. Other stuff just tastes weak, you know? This is Café Verona. I go back and forth between it, and Peets, and Death Wish.... My husband says I've turned into a coffee snob."

Tony smiled, but didn't reply... He used a blue pen to point at each part of the invoice, explaining it to her to ensure everything was correct, including their name, address, and the amount charged.

"Looks good..." She handed him a credit card from out of her phone case. *"Your boss would be very impressed with the job you did for us this morning—and with how well you walked me through everything, Tony!*

He chuckled a bit as he wrote down her credit card information on the invoice. *"That's good to hear, Mrs. Williams... I'll pat myself on the back later!"*

She looked up at him a bit confused.

"I'm the boss, ma'am. I'm just not usually out in the field anymore... but all my guys were already out on jobs, and you sounded like you needed help..."

Jenn's face lit up with surprise.

Tony took another sip of coffee, then rubbed the graying stubble on his chin.

"Oh no... I'm so sorry, Tony! I just... so YOU own Estrada Plumbing?"

He nodded, reaching down to say hello to Dooley, who had been sniffing at his ankles for a moment. Tony's right hand scratched Dooley's forehead, and then he returned his eyes to Jenn, nodding slowly. *"Been there thirty-eight years. It was my granddad's company. I was just a technician. That's all I ever wanted to be, really."*

He handed her credit card back. *"My granddad had three trucks going out each day by the time I joined him. Then less than a year later he had a heart attack..."*

"Oh... I'm so sorry..." Jenn offered.

Tony's face gathered and wrinkled as he pressed his lips together, squinted his eyes, and sighed quietly. *"Yeah. Completely unexpected. I was just a dumb kid. And I had no idea what to do when I found out he willed the business to me."*

"That sounds scary."

"Ha... you're not wrong! I had so much to learn. Wasn't even sure I'd be able to keep the doors open. But people were counting on me."

Tony adjusted himself in the stool and looked at her. He paused before delivering the next line with seriousness. *"And I only tell you all that because, well, I could help you with your work stuff."*

Now Jenn looked puzzled. She sat her mug on the counter and held it with both hands, cocking her head to the side and waiting for Tony to explain.

He tore the top invoice copy from the clipboard and slid it across the brown granite counter toward her. *"Maybe it's a good thing your call came to me today, Jenn..."*

She waited for him to continue.

"I've been thinking about what you said. What made today more challenging for you. The upsetting call with your boss that you mentioned... being worried about how you need to become a better leader..."

Jenn didn't respond. She was listening intently, though. What was this plumber talking about?

"I know exactly how you're feeling..." Tony took another sip from his mug. *"I was in the same spot. I was a good*

technician... but I knew nothing about running a business or leading people. That is a different skill set than what I had..." Now he paused a moment.

Dooley was on the couch, disinterested now.

"But I discovered those are ALL things you can learn. Somebody helped me keep the business going... and now we've got twelve trucks out running each day, because I figured out some things that might be helpful to you..."

Jenn was listening... She was curious to hear how a plumber could possibly help her. "That's nice of you, Tony. I just don't know..."

Tony smiled warmly at her suspicious expression. "So, the stuff you are stressed about with your team... it's really just like what you are dealing with here..."

Jenn leaned against the countertop and stared at him, unsure how he would connect a flooded floor and refrigerator leak to her team's challenges. Her eyebrows wrinkled down a bit as she squinted her eyes slightly with skepticism

"Okay," Tony said, as he moved back to the countertop with his clipboard. "Have you ever heard of the Ladder of Awareness?"

"No... what's that?"

Tony flipped past the duplicate invoice copies on top of his clipboard to get to the yellow tablet of blank paper underneath. He drew four lines on the page with his black pen, one on top of the other, and each one shorter than the one beneath it.

The simple four-line drawing looked like a set of steps.

"It's the first thing I had to learn as a leader. This is what explains how your water leak and your work issues are the same. See, the stuff you have to deal with and overcome as a leader is the same..."

On the bottom line of his drawing, he wrote the word **UNAWARE.**

"So, when you woke up this morning... did you know there was a leak?"

Jenn shook her head. *"No..."*

"Right, that is how everything starts. Something happens, but you are UNAWARE of it. The leak had happened sometime yesterday, but you didn't know there was a problem, so you went about your normal routine, right?"

"Yeah... okay?"

Jenn adjusted herself in the stool and sat more upright now.

"But then you came downstairs. And that is when you saw the floor was wet. That is when you called me. You saw the damage. But you didn't know where the water was coming from, right?"

She nodded slightly in agreement.

Tony wrote the word **SYMPTOM AWARE** on the next line, above UNAWARE.

He looked at her and tapped the paper with the tip of his pen. *"That is where bad leaders get stuck. They get upset. They get frustrated. They know something needs to be fixed, but they don't know what to do. Because they are just seeing the symptom. They don't know what is really causing the damage."*

Then he wrote on the next line up and turned the clipboard to let her read it. On the third line from the bottom he had written **PROBLEM AWARE**.

Jenn was still unsure how this related to her team, but she let him continue because he was clearly passionate about sharing something he felt was helpful.

"That is the difference between bad leaders and effective leaders right there!" He tipped his forehead in the direction of the clipboard on her countertop.

Jenn was clearly not as impressed as he had expected her to be.

Tony politely grabbed the clipboard and pointed to the drawing. *"Bad leaders see the symptom. They try to fix the symptom. They get distracted by the symptom... but the best leaders figure out what the problem is that created the symptom. And if you can determine what the real problem is, the last part is usually a lot easier than you expect..."*

He wrote on the top line, and turned the paper to let her read it. At the top were the words **SOLUTION AWARE**.

"Replacing the freezer line was easy. Took maybe five minutes. The challenge is finding out what was causing the leak and all the damage. But you can only implement a successful solution when you understand what the problem is..."

Jenn appreciated his enthusiasm, and she was grateful he wanted to help her. But it seemed like a pretty obvious lesson, right? And she still didn't see the connection to leading her team.

Tony appeared to notice her underwhelmed reaction. *"Mrs. Williams, I know it sounds simple... but this is a powerful idea for you to grasp as a leader. Not because of your water leak..."*

He pointed at her refrigerator. *"But because of your job. Because if you want solutions to lead more effectively, you have to understand the difference between the symptoms you are seeing and the problems that are causing them!"*

"That would be fantastic. I've definitely got a few leaks at work," Jenn said.

"Most leaders do..." Tony validated her. *"I know I did. And what I've learned over the years has helped me build a business and develop a team that I'm proud of."*

"Okay. I'm listening..." Jenn admitted.

"Those leaks you are dealing with at work..." He said, interested in her reply.

"Yeah?"

"They don't get better on their own. And the most costly and destructive issue on your team is the one you haven't addressed."

Jenn considered that a moment, more concerned after pondering the comment.

"If you are anything like I was back when I started, you want to do a good job. You just don't know how. Because nobody took the time to explain that when you take over as a leader, the things that made you great in the job you had before

aren't gonna help you with the challenges you are walking into..."

Jenn had already discovered the truth in that. She nodded her agreement.

Tony lifted his empty mug and placed it on the countertop. *"I truly appreciate the coffee, Mrs. Williams."*

"Please... It's Jenn"

"Well, Jenn. I'm glad we met." He grabbed the clipboard in his left hand and tore the paper he had drawn on from the pad. *"And I'd be happy to have another coffee with you if you'd like to accelerate your education as a leader... Believe me, experience don't make you a better leader—awareness does! Before someone stepped in as a mentor to me, my awareness came from expensive mistakes. I'm guessing you'd prefer not to go through all that?"*

Jen paused. She hadn't had a mentor before. But this was just a little too odd, right? *"I appreciate the offer, Mr. Estrada. I really do..."*

She looked down at what he had written on the yellow legal pad one more time, politely, before continuing her thought. *"But I really don't want to bother you. I'm sure I'll figure it out."*

Tony looked disappointed for a moment, then shrugged his shoulders and smiled. *"That's okay... I get it. But if you change your mind, I'm happy to talk with you about what effective leaders DO."*

He turned and made his way to the front door. Under the fabric of his shirt, she could see the bony shoulders that often come with aging. Tony opened the door and turned back to her before leaving. He tipped the top of his clipboard to her as he spoke. *"Hope your day gets better, Mrs. Williams... Nice to meet you."*

Jenn smiled as he closed the door and went to his van. And before she could get back to the couch to pick Dooley up and snuggle him, she heard her phone vibrating on the top of the granite countertop.

She frowned when she saw the name on her screen. *"Hi Dan, what's up?"* She could hear the annoyed tone in her voice.

"Morning Jenn. Sorry to call so early. But I'm, uh, working through some of the layout for the Houston project?"

Jenn's eyes rolled as she waited for Dan to continue with his complaint. *"Uh huh?"*

"Well, there's a ton that needed to be fixed. So, I'm not gonna have them by tomorrow. And I still need those measurements you were going to get from the sales team?"

Jenn thought about the conversation she had earlier with Lewis. This was not good. Dan had been a bit rude and was dragging his feet with his work recently... and this last-minute delay was not helpful. *"Dan, that's not a bomb we can drop on manufacturing OR the client at this point. We've got a timeline. You've known about that!"*

"Well, that's the situation. Get those updated measurements to me, I'll do what I can." His voice was angry.

But she was the one who should be upset, right? *"You're just NOW figuring this out? DAN?"*

"That's all I can tell you, Jenn. You wanted to be the one that handled reaching out to sales for the updated numbers."

"But Dan... You can't..." She heard the line go dead. Dammit.

She put her phone down on the counter and looked around her home. There was gray concrete where her carpet had been just last night. Her furniture was sitting on tiny Styrofoam blocks to keep it dry.

She breathed in slowly and exhaled. Dooley looked at her with an unchanged dog-grin from the couch.

Brian was in another country. And she needed to figure out what to do to keep her job. She needed to deal with Maria and Dan... and somehow get her team on the same page. But she didn't know what that actually looked like.

Jenn pressed her lips together, breathed out through her nose, and picked up her phone again. Her thumb pressed the screen a few times, and she lifted it to her ear. *"You still willing to take on a new student?"*

From the other end of the line, Tony's warm voice answered. *"Yes ma'am! If you're available tomorrow morning at 7:00, I know a place we can talk over a great cup of coffee..."*

EFFECTIVE
— L E A D E R S —

CHAPTER 3

THE CYCLE OF CULTURE

Jenn recalled passing by the Deja-Brew Coffee Shop a few times previously in her car, but this was the first time she had been inside.

The place was pretty busy, and had a warm, comfortable design with lots of pastels and poofy chairs. A few people were in line at the counter, and many were scattered among the tables, with mugs of assorted colors in their hands or beside their laptops.

Large pictures of coffee with cute puns hung on every wall. She smiled at the one that said "The ends justify the beans" across from her.

There was a low hum of music underneath the customer conversations, and the entire place had a fun energy. The employees behind the counter seemed to enjoy working there, greeting customers with enthusiasm.

Jenn ordered a simple large dark roast, black, and carried it to a table with two chairs in the front corner of the store.

She had gotten there well before seven am, partly because she was curious to hear what Tony would share... and partly because worrying about her job had kept her from sleeping well.

Jenn had talked with Brian before she went to bed, and that had been nice.

But Brian wasn't able to solve the issues she had on her team. He had his own hands full working with the players he was trying to coach.

Jenn walked Dooley early, waited impatiently for him to do his business, and hurried to the location Tony had suggested, not knowing what to expect from their chat.

At least the coffee was good!

She peeked over the rim of her heavy yellow Deja-Brew-logoed mug and spotted Tony walking in.

He had on a similar outfit as he had worn the day before, but his shirt was navy blue instead of black. He hurried over to her with a new red spiral bound notebook in his hand, and placed it on the small round table in front of her. *"You have a pen?"*

"Yep!" Jenn said, pulling one from her purse. *"I came prepared."*

"Terrific." He said, and sat down at the table. *"So, I'm curious. Before I start, tell me what seem to be your main problems now at work?"*

Guess he's not having coffee? Jenn thought. Am I really going to share my problems with this plumber?

He was attentive, waiting for her to talk, and seemed genuinely interested. Okay, then. Might as well tell him, she thought. What do I have to lose?

She peeked down at the notebook, then back at him, and started talking.

She covered her unexpected promotion, her lack of experience as a manager, her team's performance problems, her issues with Maria being distant, Dan being rude, the projects they were preparing plans for, Brian being away for another twelve days in Spain, and everything else worrying her recently...

Tony nodded with empathy for all it. He allowed her to unload her cargo of concerns and emotions without judgment.

And just as Jenn finished her list of troubles, a young woman with long black hair walked over with a fresh hot mug of coffee and placed it on the table in front of him.

"Hey Papi!" The woman had on a black t-shirt with the white Deja-Brew logo on it. Then she kissed Tony lovingly on his scruffy cheek.

"Lucia! Good morning. And thank you." Tony sipped from the bright-green logoed mug and placed it on the table. *"Oh, this is my friend Jenn..."* He motioned with his hand as an introduction. *"Jenn, I am pleased to introduce my daughter Lucia. She owns this little business!"*

Lucia nodded, waved, and smiled, but returned to where she was needed, serving customers behind the counter. On the back of Lucia's t-shirt as she walked away, Jenn could read the playful yellow font that said - "yawns are silent screams for coffee!"

Jenn smirked and looked to Tony. *"So, I get why you wanted to meet here!"*

"Well, yes. It is an added benefit to support my daughter when I am teaching..." He touched the notebook with his index finger. *"But we are here for you!"*

Jenn sat back in her chair, anticipating his forthcoming wisdom. *"Okay. Well, now you know what I'm dealing with, I'm ready to hear your advice. What do you have for me?"*

Tony smiled warmly. He sipped from his mug, then reached out and opened up the red notebook resting in front of Jenn to its first blank lined page. *"I brought this for you to write down the things we talk about. You will want to record as much as possible, because you will return to it in the future to remind yourself of the things I share. And in time, you'll discover greater appreciation for the things we discuss that at first may not seem as relevant..."*

His tone was like a calm and encouraging professor. *"I'll be giving you a crash course on what effective leaders do to build a more productive culture over a few good cups of coffee. And you are free to apply and implement whatever you think fits your needs. That notebook will be your timeless buffet of business wisdom that you can use... and even add to later..."* Tony paused, then added *"It's like reading King Lear... I find something new each time I read it."*

She noticed the age in his deep raspy voice as he spoke slowly and intentionally to her. He had the deliberate voice of a man who had shared these ideas before, and he clearly wanted to help her.

Jenn grabbed the pen and clicked it open. She wrote the date in the top right-hand corner... 8/17.

Tony leaned in and tilted his head playfully. *"Ready?"*

Jenn noticed his eyebrows lift. They were a tangle of gray and black, just like his beard.

She took note of the bustling collection of customers and reassured herself that she felt comfortable in this place. *"Yep. Properly caffeinated and sincerely curious!"*

"Okay, good. The truest sign of a commitment to growth is asking for help. Being coachable is the first step to being more successful!" Tony sipped his coffee and sat straighter in his chair. *"Improvement requires us to care more about our results than our pride... and people are most coachable when they are desperate from failure or struggles. So I am glad to meet with you, because your struggles have made you coachable. But I must admit, though, that for me to share the lessons to make you a more effective leader, we will need to meet for more than just one coffee. It will probably take five or six..."*

"Meetings or cups?" Jenn asked.

Tony looked confused.

Jenn explained with a grin. *"Sorry... just being funny."*

"Oh," Tony said. *"I meant meetings. Ha... yes,"* he smiled, *"it will probably take us more than six cups of coffee to get through what I hope to share..."*

Jenn shrugged. *"Okay, I could meet most any morning. It's just me and my dog for the next two weeks... and if we're done before eight, that won't interfere with any meetings."*

"Okay, that is good." He finished the remaining coffee in his mug and turned his head, seeming to search for his daughter. Jenn's mug was still half full, and she waited with a pen at the ready to record whatever golden nuggets Tony was willing to provide.

He turned back to her and began again. *"Yes, mornings at seven are good for me too. So after today, we can meet tomorrow, then Friday. And the same next week, if that is suitable?"*

"Got it. Today, Wednesday, Friday, and the same next week. I'll be here by seven... should I expect to fill up this notebook?"

Tony nodded one time to confirm their agreement. *"There are four main lessons I will share to help you be a more effective leader. Each involves four steps that you will need to understand..."*

"Got it - Four lessons, four steps..."

Tony continued. *"I'll try to remind you to write down certain things, but you will find that details are helpful, and notebooks always remember much better than we can."* He tapped the side of his head with an index finger. *"So, let's begin with what I explained when I visited you yesterday for the leak. Do you recall what I said about awareness, and how it affects the growth of a leader?"*

"I think so..."

"Good. That's where we will start. Take a moment and write down the four stages of awareness on the first page of your notebook, there—"

Jenn drew four lines, one above the next.

On the bottom she wrote **unaware**. Above that she wrote **symptom aware.**

Above that was **problem aware.**

And on the top line she wrote **solution aware.**

Tony pointed down at the page as she wrote. *"That is the first lesson on what effective leaders do – and the foundation for everything else we will discuss. Leaders do not get better because they get older or more experienced. Awareness is the key to your success. Not just in growing yourself, but in building a culture where your people can thrive."*

Jenn nodded as she wrote.

Tony paused to wait for her to finish getting her thought onto the page. *"Do you know what leadership is, Jenn?"*

She looked at him, considering her reply. *"Well, yeah. It's being in charge. Being responsible... Being the boss, right?"*

Tony chuckled. *"Yes, that is often part of it. But I have found that leadership is less about your position and more about your influence. You can lead without the authority of a title. So the definition I like is this...* **Leadership is the influence our interactions have on the behavior of others."**

Jenn considered his insight. It made sense. Jenn had seen people have a significant impact on others, even if they didn't have the authority of a leadership position. Both for good and bad. She nodded slowly and wrote down what he had said.

Tony continued. *"Your role or position comes with certain responsibilities and resources, but leadership is skill, not a position. And if leadership is the influence of the interactions you have, then* **your awareness affects the quality of those interactions."**

He paused and watched her to be sure she had gotten that last part down on the page. She did. *"I'm glad you wrote both of those comments down, Jenn."*

"A notebook's job is to remember the important stuff for me, right?"

"Exactly. It will serve you in growing your awareness. You see, when you are put in the role of a manager or leader, the most important thing you need to be aware of is the CULTURE that you are allowing or creating. **In every organization, culture is always a symptom of leadership."**

Hearing this, Jenn placed the notebook down on the table and leaned back into her chair, palms in her lap, looking off to the side to digest it.

Tony allowed her to sit in thought for a few moments, then redirected her attention. *"Think later. DO later... But be sure the idea is not lost."* He pointed at her notebook. *"Culture... is... always... a symptom... of leadership. Good. So, culture is what you must focus on if you want results and retention. Talent is important. Every team needs talent. Strategy is important. Every team needs strategy. But culture always determines how well your talent will implement your strategy..."*

He paused for only a second, chuckling to himself as if he had just remembered to share something that many people misunderstood. *"But do not be distracted. Culture is not the snacks, the perks, or the time off that you provide your people. **Culture is simply the sum of behaviors you allow to be repeated on your team.**"*

Jenn flipped the page and wrote his entire last sentence on the top of the second page in her notebook. She didn't yet know how this stuff would help her with Maria or Dan or her team... but she was excited to hear and consider it. She knew they were valuable insights. But she felt like they were 10,000 feet above where she needed to be operating.

Tony looked at his watch. *"Okay, the last two things we will talk about today are the cycle of culture and the matrix of interactions. We should have time for both. Maybe one page for each. You ready?"*

Jenn had not taken notes like this since college. She certainly hadn't expected a coffee conversation to be like this. It wasn't even really a conversation. It was a lecture. A monologue. And probably a helpful one. But it was not what she had anticipated when she met Tony just a day ago.

She turned the page and wrote "**Cycle of Culture**" across the top. Then she waited for him to resume teaching.

Tony gave her a thumbs up and a wrinkled warm smile. *"Okay, Jenn. So... if culture is about repeated behaviors, how do we change them? What is it that will shift the behaviors of others? That was a difficult question for me early on, and that is the first thing I learned from my first mentor, my Tia Lena..."*

He smiled and sat up a bit straighter as he remembered her. *"She was a manager in a small credit union. Without her, our plumbing business would have failed for sure. Here is what she taught me about culture..."*

He motioned to ask for the pen, and then leaned forward over the table and drew a circle in the middle of the page.

At the top of the circle, he wrote "**Experiences**."

On the right side, he wrote "**Awareness**"

On the bottom, he wrote "**Beliefs**"

And on the left side he wrote "**Behaviors**."

He handed the pen back to her and pointed his index finger at the left side of the circle. *"Remember how I said culture is the sum of behaviors allowed and repeated on your team?"*

Jenn nodded, and adjusted the pen in her hand to have it ready.

*"Those behaviors become what you and your team experience as culture. But here is the interesting thing: People can have the same experience, and come away from it remembering things very differently. So, **awareness is what we notice in our experiences...**"*

He pointed at each word he had written around the circle as he talked. *"That awareness is what creates the beliefs we carry... and those beliefs are what drive our behaviors. Does that make sense?"*

"Yes, it does," she replied. She let her eyes follow the cycle

around the circle on the page again, quietly, to be sure she had the concept clearly in her mind.

"So, the CULTURE you build - and the results you see from your team - ultimately come down to how effective YOUR BEHAVIORS are as a leader. Your interactions are very important to your team. And those interactions are affected by your BELIEFS – the stories you tell yourself..."

He paused to let her get those ideas onto the notebook paper. *"Those beliefs are shaped by your AWARENESS... And remember, awareness is what you notice and learn from your EXPERIENCES. Understanding the cycle of culture is the key to becoming more effective as a leader - and I've shared it a few times with others... But eventually I realized the model is incomplete."*

He paused, but not long enough for her to respond. As he did, he pointed at the coiled metal spine of her notebook. *"Culture is not just a flat cycle... It's dynamic... It either gets better or worse. So, culture is really... kinda like a SLINKY. It can spiral up... or spiral down, based on the interactions we have as a leader."*

Jenn finished writing and looked up at him.

Her body was still hunched over the open notebook, one forearm resting on the table.

"Okay, Tony. This is a lot..." She sat upright and held out her hands, palms up.

"But how does it fix the leaks I'm seeing with my team?"

Before Tony could respond, Lucia returned, smiling. *"Anything else I can get you two?"* She stood between them at the table, and her eyes went first to Tony and then to Jenn. *"Bet your wrist is sore with all that writing!"* she said, smiling. She had her father's easy warmth.

Tony shook his hand in the air. *"Nothing more for me, thanks. Um, Jenn, I've only got one more thing to share with you today... would you like another coffee?"*

Jenn shook her head. *"No, thank you. But it was excellent. I look forward to coming back!"*

Lucia touched her dad's shoulder and then left them to their conversation.

Tony turned his attention back to Jenn's question, facing her. *"That is a smart question, Jenn. And yes, we will be discussing many specific actions you can implement with your team. But it is helpful to see and understand the bigger picture before you zoom in and talk about specific tactics!"*

He pointed at the notebook to encourage her to be ready to write again. *"Much of our time to come will focus on certain things you can do. But it is valuable to know the why behind the what. Today, you get a foundation for all that we will discuss in our future conversations. And, yes - we will end with something specific that you can take away from our chat to be a better leader..."*

She nodded in appreciation, and readied her pen.

"So today we have discussed the Ladder of Awareness. And we also talked about awareness as a key part of the cycle of culture that you, in a position of authority, are responsible for building and sustaining. And I explained that culture is always a symptom of your leadership. All of which brings us to the last

thing I will share with you this morning, which will determine the quality of your interactions…"

Yes, Jenn thought, that is a good summary. But what will I do differently because of our time today? She wasn't sure yet.

Tony looked around the room and motioned at the many people that surrounded them in the coffee shop. It was a diverse group. *"Jenn, when you ask people what makes their leader great, they don't talk about wild ideas, big personalities, or fantastic successes…. They talk about small daily interactions where their leader truly sees, hears, and values them."*

He now looked directly at her. *"And so, if you want to be a better leader, your job is to have more productive interactions that influence the people you depend on and care about, yes?"*

He didn't wait for her reply. Instead, he pointed his finger in the sky, as if he had just had an important thought. He reached out politely to request her pen, which she gave him.

He drew a cross in the middle of the next blank page of her notebook. One line was vertical, the other horizontal. And he tapped the pen in each of the four quadrants.

Then, in the bottom left area, he wrote the word **plain.**

In the bottom right corner, he wrote the word **pointed.**

In the top left corner, he wrote the word **pleasant.**

And in the top right corner, he wrote the word **productive.**

"Imagine," he said, pointing at the page with her pen, *"that this side, here on the left, is about how considerate you are*

when you talk with your team. It is focused on how much effort you give to being kind and polite. Plain is not very considerate, but on the top left, pleasant interactions are very considerate, yes?"

He nodded as he asked, and she dutifully nodded along with him. *"Across the bottom of the chart is how compelling you are in getting people to take action as a result of your communication. It is focused on getting people to do something. On the bottom left, plain interactions are not very compelling. And on the bottom right you have pointed conversations, which are focused on getting them to do something, but not very considerate."*

He then circled the word **productive**, and kindly offered the pen back to her. *"That is what you must aim for. The productive interactions that effective leaders have are both considerate and compelling. That means your next great leadership act is always a productive interaction where you are intentional about both!"*

INTERACTION MATRIX FOR EFFECTIVE LEADERS

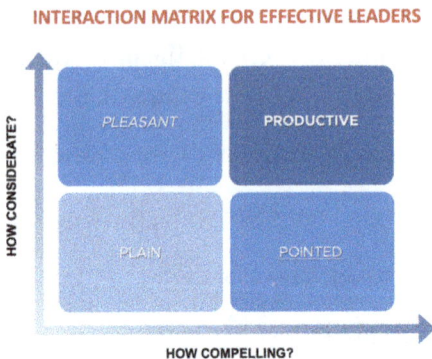

Tony leaned forward awkwardly, reaching his right hand to grab something from his back pocket. When his hand returned, it held a silver adjustable wrench. He lifted the wrench up to about eye level and shook it reverently in the air. *"This wrench is the reminder I have always kept in my pocket to help me be more productive in my conversations with people."*

He placed it on the table next to his empty green mug. *"It was a gift from my dad, because I was slow to understand that it was my responsibility to adjust to my clients and coworkers if I wanted better interactions. That is the thing I hope you will think about and work on first."*

Jenn looked at the adjustable wrench he had placed on the table for emphasis. She hadn't really adjusted much to her team. That was true. But wasn't it their job to adjust to her?

As she studied the drawing Tony had made in her notebook, she wondered which quadrant would define most of her recent conversations with her team. She had definitely been more pointed, she thought. Maybe too pointed, and not considerate enough to be productive? *"Looks simple. But not as easy as it looks I guess..."* she said.

"That is your assignment for today, then. In your interactions, be more intentional and aware of how you interact with your team. The quality of your interactions with talent is even more important than the quality of the talent on your team - because the interactions you have determine how your people feel and perform each day!"

He rose from his chair and looked at his watch. *"Think of*

what it feels like to be led by you, based on those interactions. And I will meet you back here tomorrow at seven!"

Jenn closed the notebook, and stood to shake his hand. *"Thanks for this first conversation, Tony. I really didn't know what to expect, but I am looking forward to hearing more."*

Tony finished shaking her hand, then turned to wave at his daughter before leaving.

Jenn stayed behind and sat down again for a moment. She turned her mug up to empty it of the last gulp of room temperature coffee that remained, and considered what Tony had shared today.

Interesting.

She was glad to have heard his ideas on culture and leadership, and the importance of her interactions in influencing her team to perform better. But there were still a lot of leaks on her team that needed to be fixed. Talking about a cycle of culture wasn't going to get Dan to finish updating those plans.

She waved a polite goodbye to Lucia as she left, and turned her attention back to the office. Today was Tuesday. Everyone would be on-site instead of working from home. It was a great opportunity to see all six of her team members – Chris, Brandon, Maria, Dan, Justin, and Tanya.

She still wanted to find out why Maria had been a no show for their video call yesterday, and had not replied to her emails.

She wanted to be sure she got Dan the updated measurements he needed for the Houston project. And she wanted to make sure everyone knew how important the next few weeks of productivity were to her.

She should have had one of those muffins from Deja Brew. She felt her stomach turning. And whether it was from a lack of breakfast, or from her anxiety about her job and team, she was very unsure what to expect from her day today.

EFFECTIVE
— L E A D E R S —

CHAPTER 4

ASSUMPTIONS

The door at Deja Brew flew open violently. It even surprised one of the customers... In her haste to get in from the rain, Jenn had pushed it with more strength than she had realized. It was 7:03 and she was angry at herself. She prided herself on not being late.

She had texted Tony on her drive in to let him know she was on the way, but that didn't remove her self-critical voice from gnawing at her and making the ride in both more dangerous and more miserable than it should have been.

Jenn collected herself with a heavy sigh and scanned the interior of the coffee shop. She found Tony's warm smile and waving hand beckoning her to join him at a table on the other side of the room from where they sat the day before.

She had the red spiral bound notebook in her left hand, a small brown leather purse hanging from her right shoulder, and a few droplets fell from her head when she shook it in exasperation as an apology as she walked over to him. *"Thank you for your patience, Tony. This is truly a priority for me, and I want you to know I value your time... What a crazy morning."*

Jenn placed the notebook on the table between them, dropped her purse gently on the floor beside her chair, and was met by a waitress with a napkin in her hand standing next to the table when she looked back up. Jenn accepted the offered napkin and dabbed away the rain from her face.

"Can I get you anything?"

Jenn smiled in appreciation. *"Yes, thank you! Dark roast. Black."*

The waitress disappeared, and Jenn finally gave her attention back to Tony, who shared his usual warm, understanding grin. *"Everything okay?"* Tony asked.

Hundreds of tiny droplets of rain raced down the outside of the large front window that looked out onto the street, and the soft pattering sound it made became muffled background noise for the morning's coffee conversation.

"Oh, yes. Just more office drama. Guess the weather is appropriate considering how I feel about my team right now..."

Tony raised his eyebrows to invite an explanation.

Jenn sighed. *"Two of my people are just lazy and irresponsible. And one insists on being rude and disrespectful to me, even though I took on extra work to ensure we had accurate updated measurements for an important project."* She stopped her rant, adjusted her body in the chair, and looked across at Tony. *"But I am glad to be here, now..."*

Tony took a sip of coffee from his oversized blue Deja-Brew Mug, and spread his hands open, palms up, after placing it back on the table. *"Wonderful. It sounds like today's topic will be very helpful for you."*

Tony pointed at her red spiral notebook, which was still unopened. *"Are you ready to get started?"*

Jenn leaned over to reach into her purse for a pen, opened the notebook to its first blank page, and wrote the date at the top of it. 8/18. *"Ready. And I reviewed yesterday's notes last night again. The Ladder of Awareness is about looking past symptoms to find the real problem you need to solve. And that led us to the Cycle of Culture, where you explained how culture is nothing more than behaviors... and behaviors are driven by our beliefs... and those beliefs are a result of our awareness, which is what we notice in our experiences..."* She looked up with a proud smile, seeking his validation for a successful review.

"And?"

Jenn hesitated. *"Right. AND the thing you shared about leadership being the influence of our interactions on others... You gave me the Interaction Matrix and wanted me to focus on productive interactions by being both considerate and compelling!"* Again, she looked up expecting praise.

"And...?" Tony moved his right hand to his back pocket and tapped his hip, head tilted, and eyebrows lifted as an encouraging prompt.

"Oh, goodness. And you explained that leaders need to be like a wrench, and adjust ourselves to work better with every client or coworker."

"Terrific. And now we move on to our second major lesson. Assumptions..."

He paused and looked away from her, interrupted by a waitress who had arrived with a bright yellow mug. Steam rose from the dark coffee that swirled inside and nearly escaped the rim of the mug as it was placed on the table.

Jenn let it sit, allowing it to cool before picking it up. She nodded respectfully to Tony, pen still in her hand, and he continued.

"Just as there were four levels of awareness, and four parts to the culture cycle we discussed, there are four assumptions that leaders must challenge to become more effective. Like you, I did not know this when I first transitioned to being a manager. My team would have appreciated it very much if I had!"

He pointed to the waiting blank page in her notebook. *"Four areas of assumptions we will talk about today. The first is PURPOSE. Above that, PRINCIPLES. Above that, PEOPLE. And above that is POLITENESS."*

Jenn wrote them down and listened for Tony to continue.

"Next to purpose, write how you define success. Next to principles, write values and expectations. Next to people, write the stories you tell. And at the top, next to politeness, write down that nice is unkind."

He watched her do as he had suggested.

NICE IS UNKIND	POLITENESS
THE STORIES YOU TELL	PEOPLE
VALUES AND EXPECTATIONS	PRINCIPLES
HOW YOU DEFINE SUCCESS	PURPOSE

"So, the first step in overcoming harmful assumptions is understanding your purpose. This was hard for me, and I feel it may be a similar challenge for you, Jenn..."

He sat back in his chair as he explained... *"Like you, I had to learn the difference between what made me successful as a plumber and the things that would make me successful as a leader. It was easy for me to do everything myself when I was out in my van on house calls, but it was much harder to figure out what it took to build a culture where others could do what I used to."*

Tony looked across the table to check Jenn's attention. She was listening closely. *"Most leaders get promoted because they are really good at giving the right answers - so they think that in their new role as leader, they have to keep on giving right answers... and that is impossible to sustain. You will get burned out from trying to do things yourself, or you get frustrated trying to convince people you know everything you think you should. Effective leaders understand that the promotion requires a shift, from giving right answers to asking better questions. Effective leaders figure out that success in their new role is less about technical skills and more about interpersonal skills... because getting stuff done as a leader means we have to work through other people."*

Tony watched as she wrote, breathing slowly with his hands clasped together. *"All the breakthroughs I've had as a leader came from realizing that something I thought I knew turned out to be untrue... and the most important assumption I had to challenge was my belief that I was responsible for deadlines and deliverables instead of team results and retention."*

He paused and leaned forward again, reaching for his mug of coffee. *"So, think about how you have been defining success. Has it been about managing every detail, demanding perfection, and complaining if they don't work the same way you did? Or have you been focused on caring about, encouraging, developing, and supporting the imperfect people it is your job to serve?"*

He sat back again to give her time to consider the question.

She reached for her mug and sipped quietly as she thought about it. Then on the page, she wrote in large letters: "serve, support, care about, and develop the people responsible for team results".

"Good. And once you understand your real purpose as a leader, you can shift your attention to assumptions about the principles that define how your team should work together. Every business or team comes together for a reason - that mission is something that everyone is trying to contribute to achieving. For me, it was creating happy customers by solving their plumbing problems.

But that mission is not enough. Because sometimes we can sabotage that goal as leaders if we don't take time to ensure everyone is clear on values and expectations. Assuming that people know what you expect, without being clear and sharing examples, is almost certainly going to lead to misunderstandings and frustrations...

Values and clear expectations are like guardrails for our people - they keep us moving forward safely in the same direction. But if you don't have firm guardrails, people will go off road and cause damage to their coworkers or clients."

Jenn smiled and seemed to shrug off the issue of values. *"Oh, well we have already identified our company values. They're on our website, and part of the onboarding packet that everyone on the team gets."*

Tony shook his head, confident she had not understood what he was getting at. *"That is the costly assumption that most leaders make, Jenn. And it is often the reason teams get frustrated or confused. Let me do something with you that I learned to do with every member of my team, okay?"*

Jenn nodded, curious.

Tony leaned over and flipped the page of her notebook and pointed to the back of the one she had been writing on earlier. *"I used to use index cards for this activity, and we would do it in a team meeting with everyone together... but today we will improvise. So, take a moment and write down the values that everyone at ModernSpace Workstations should be familiar with."*

He waited as she wrote down the words.

She took an extra few moments to recall the last of the four that she recalled being displayed on the company website. They had also been on a poster in the office breakroom, but she only went in once a week and hadn't looked at it in a while.

On the page, she had written responsiveness, integrity, teamwork, and improvement.

"Great. So now write down a specific example of what each one of those looks like on your team, in your hallways or offices."

He finished his coffee while she was writing out the examples she imagined.

"Now, we don't have the rest of your team here... but I'm guessing that what THEY would have written down might be different from what you have on your paper. What do you think?"

Jenn had to admit that her idea of each of the words was probably not the same as what the other six people on her team would have written. *"Okay. I understand. You can't assume other people are thinking what you do."*

"Especially when it comes to values, Jenn," Tony added. *"After getting clear on your team mission, they are the most important thing you can get clear on - because you want your people to take initiative. Getting clear about your team values helps you as a leader feel better about giving them freedom to make decisions. But values are only helpful if you and your team have discussed what they look like as specific behaviors. Then they are more aware of what is exceptional, what is acceptable, and what is unacceptable."*

Tony stopped speaking and pointed at the wall behind her. There was a large colourful drawing of a coffee mug behind a quote: Keep your hands up - we mug our customers!

"I've noticed many companies think they have values figured out because they hang a nice poster. But words on walls or websites don't drive behaviors... example is the greatest tool for that. And you only prove your commitment to the values you've chosen when you are willing to let go of clients or colleagues who violate them."

Jenn wrote as he spoke, getting down on the page, a reminder to herself to go through this with her team sometime soon.

When she stopped writing and looked up, Tony clapped his hands together once with unexpected enthusiasm. *"And now we can talk about the assumption you made when you first came in today..."*

Jenn thought back to earlier, coming in from the rain. It was still gray and overcast outside now, but the drizzle has subsided.

"So, we covered the dangers of assumptions about purpose and assumptions about principles. The third assumption you need to guard against is about your people."

He pointed to where he had written the word people on the previous page. *"Remember when you described the people on your team as lazy and irresponsible? Or as rude and disrespectful?"*

Jenn was embarrassed. Yes, of course, she had said it... but she was still emotional from their email messages and conversations - and disappointed in their lack of professionalism.

Tony held his palms out toward her. *"No need to be defensive. We have all done it. Believe me! I was the worst when I started. But it can hurt your team a lot when you make assumptions about them... because when we lack information, we often default to negative stories."*

Jenn hadn't moved. She was listening, but still felt a bit chided.

"It's okay... the truth is that we all tell ourselves stories about the people on our team. But we have to be careful not to hold onto a story that isn't true. So, I want to give you a question that you can ask yourself when you feel you might be telling a story about someone that might not be productive. Ready?"

Jenn nodded, pen ready.

"WHAT EVIDENCE DO I HAVE TO SUPPORT THIS STORY... AND WHAT OTHER REASONS MIGHT HELP EXPLAIN THE SAME BEHAVIOR?"

Jenn wrote the question down in her notebook. Then she let the pen fall noiselessly to the table as she contemplated it.

Tony gave her time to process the question.

Around them, there was still the busy movement of employees and customers, and the faint hum of music in the background. But Jenn was lost in her thoughts, staring blankly at the page...

"Beliefs are the roads we travel on. If we believe someone is lazy, then each experience becomes evidence to support our belief and send us down the same road to the same frustrating and cynical destination - and that affects our interactions with that person. Maybe that is what has happened with the people on your team recently?

"Sometimes our beliefs are precisely what keep us from accomplishing the results we want, because we continue to look for evidence to support an assumption instead of examining the assumption itself. One common assumption is that everyone should be like and think like you... but different personality styles and backgrounds can be beneficial. We just have to believe they are an asset, not a threat."

Tony tapped the table with his index finger for emphasis. *"Without examining your beliefs, you won't know which one is sabotaging progress. Beliefs direct our default behaviors and become the ruts we get into that keep us from traveling to new destinations or achievements...*

"How you see the world... how you see your people... determines how you choose to interact with them - and how much of them you get to experience. Most people protect the assumptions they have, rather than questioning or improving them. They even twist evidence to support their assumption, rather than staying coachable and curious.

"But you are someone who wants to be better. And your commitment to learning, listening, and considering these things will be the reason you become more effective in your role, Jenn."

Tony smiled warmly at her across the table, pointing an index finger at himself. *"I know this, because I spent far too* long believing unproductive things about people, but things started to change when I considered those assumptions. Remember, experience is what happens around us. Awareness is what we notice. Our beliefs are the stories we tell ourselves to interpret the things we noticed. And our behaviors are what we choose to do based on those beliefs. So, the actions of the people you came in complaining about... are there other reasons that would explain their behavior?"

Jenn wrote.

He watched.

Before she looked up, she placed the pen on the last page she had nearly filled with her notes, and rubbed the palm of her right hand with her left thumb. *"Wish I had heard this before this morning."*

Tony smiled. His eyes wrinkled into slits as he shrugged his shoulders. *"We all wish we had learned and listened better in our past. The things we regret most are not our stories, but the hurtful things we said or did inspired by those false assumptions."*

Jenn tilted her head to the side, thinking of her most recent interactions with her two "problem employees," Dan and Maria.

Maria she still had not had a real conversation with. She had sent Jenn an email apologizing for missing their meeting, but had not responded to Jenn's request for a new one to review her work activity. And she had been late with her last set of design plans. All that after ghosting Jenn for that Monday morning Zoom call, just before the discovery of the flood in her kitchen.

Of course, Dan was a different story. He was a worker, that was not the issue. But he had seemed so rude recently. And Jenn had taken that as an attack on her leadership, thinking he was treating her poorly because he didn't respect her.

Jenn looked to Tony as she returned her thoughts to the present. *"Well, I suppose I can be grateful that I didn't yell at either of them and make things worse that way..."*

"Questioning your assumptions about people can keep you from telling false stories about their behaviors. But if we are not curious... if we do not get clarity about what truly was the reason for their behaviors, then the behaviors do not improve. Have you asked the people that upset you about their behaviors?"

Jenn shook her head. *"One team member, Maria... I haven't talked to her at all. She's been unresponsive on email the last day or two. And Dan, the other one I'm bothered by, I didn't say anything to him about his tone on the phone this morning. I didn't want to make things worse, you know?"*

Tony gave a slow nod, as if turning a wrench in his mind. *"Ah. You were being nice."*

Jenn frowned. *"Well, isn't that a good thing?"*

Tony chuckled. *"Not always, Jenn. There's a big difference between being nice and being kind..."*

He wrinkled his lips together, as he paused. He seemed to be searching for what to say next... then he continued. *"Remember when I found that tiny crack in the pipe behind your refrigerator? If I had just ignored it because I didn't want* to upset you as the homeowner, what would have happened when the water was turned back on?"

Jenn sighed. *"Things would get flooded again."*

"Exactly," Tony said. *"Being nice would mean pretending the crack isn't there. Being kind means pointing it out and fixing it before the system fails and the house is flooded. The same goes for leadership. You think you're protecting people by avoiding tough conversations, but what you're really doing is letting small problems turn into big ones."*

Jenn crossed her arms. *"So, you're saying I should've called him out?"*

Tony shook his head. *"I'm saying you should've called him up. Big difference. A kind leader doesn't ignore issues. They care enough to address them. They give honest feedback. They challenge people to be better, even when it's uncomfortable."*

He grabbed her pen and wrote into her notebook:

N.I.C.E. =
Neglected Issues Crippling Excellence

"Being 'nice' might feel good in the moment, but it's toxic to your team. If you ignore problems, avoid setting clear expectations, or excuse poor performance, you're not helping anyone - you're holding them back."

Jenn exhaled, running a hand through her hair. *"So, how do I fix it?"*

Tony smiled. *"You lead with kindness. That means saying what needs to be said, even when it's hard. It means helping people see their blind spots so they can improve. It means pushing for excellence instead of enabling mediocrity."*

Jenn nodded slowly. *"I think I get it."*

Tony clapped her on the shoulder. *"Good. Because the best leaders aren't just nice. They're kind. And that's what makes all the difference."*

He glanced down at his watch. *"We covered a good bit today. I hope it's not been too much too fast?"*

Jenn closed the red spiral notebook. *"No... honestly, I've enjoyed our chats more than I first expected. I'm learning a lot, Tony. Thank you. And I'd really like to do something for you in return..."*

Tony held a hand up and shook his head. *"Not doing this for money - but to thank the people who helped me when I needed it..."*

He began to get up from his chair, and then stopped as an idea seemed to grab him. *"Did you say your husband is a basketball coach?"*

"Yes... but he's away with the team until the end of next week."

"And they will have games nearby when the team returns?" he asked.

"Oh, yes. Their first game of the season is in October."

Tony held up an index finger and shook it triumphantly by his ear. *"Then I have an idea. My grandson loves basketball. He is nine years old... and if your husband could get us tickets so he could see a game of college teams, that would be a wonderful experience for him!"*

"Tony, I think we can make that happen! I'll talk with my husband about it."

Tony stood up to leave and held out his hand to shake hers. *"Good. And I'd like to introduce you to my son at our next morning meeting. I think he will be able to share better than I can the importance of our next conversation."*

CHAPTER 5

GETTING PAST STUFF

Tony wasn't alone. Beside him at the same small table they had occupied on Wednesday morning, when she had arrived three minutes late, was another man.

The second man was younger than Tony. He had a full head of dark black hair, parted on one side and mussed a bit on top, and wore a powder blue blazer. In front of him was half a large blueberry muffin and a yellow mug of coffee.

When Tony looked up at her, the younger man rose and extended his hand. *"Hello, I'm Roberto. It is a pleasure to meet you, Jenn!"*

Jenn smiled and greeted him, and they all sat down.

"You are early today!" Tony announced, looking at his watch. *"It's only 6:52!"*

Jenn nodded. *"Made sure to get the dog walked and myself*

together so I wasn't late again. Helped to not have the rain. And no disappointing emails in my inbox when I woke up!"

Tony got up and stood behind Roberto. *"I'll go get you a coffee, and you two can talk. I think Roberto is much better to share the value of our third lesson!"*

Roberto rolled his eyes playfully and mouthed to Jenn, "*Don't believe him*", with a grin Tony couldn't see from behind him.

Tony patted Roberto on the shoulder, and walked away towards the counter.

"Okay... So, um, I guess before I start, you need to know a little about me..."

Jenn opened her spiral red notebook onto the table and took a pen from her purse as he spoke. He had a nose sharper and more pronounced than Tony's, and he was clean shaven, but Roberto had the same warm and thoughtful eyes.

He adjusted the sleeve of his white shirt that peeked out from inside his sport coat. *"So, I did not want to be a plumber. That didn't bother dad... but he made sure to tell my sister and me both all about what he's been talking to you about. The stuff he had learned that helped him keep the business growing he knew would help us... no matter what kind of team we worked with..."*

Roberto made a helicopter sign with his right index finger, rotating it to allude to his sister's coffee shop. *"And I guess it worked. Lucia has done well here, and I am doing pretty well in my job, too. I'm an administrator at Marshall Academy."*

He tore a piece of the muffin off and popped it into his mouth, giving her time to place the reference. Marshall Academy was a well-established private school in the area that Jenn could probably not afford to send her kids to if she and Brian had any.

"Okay..."

Roberto finished chewing and continued. *"But I've only been an administrator for a couple of years. I taught history there when I started. Was in the classroom for nine years before they asked me to consider administration. And that's why dad wanted me to talk with you..."*

Jenn nodded, signaling him to go on.

"So, I guess you already covered the first two lessons he likes to share - the Ladder of Awareness and the Danger of Assumptions, right?"

Jenn pointed at her notebook, which had over a third of the pages already filled with her handwriting and a few diagrams.

Roberto grinned, showing his white top row of teeth and a dimple. *"Good. So, the third thing he talks about is what he calls the Evolution of Focus..."*

Jenn wrote that at the top of the next blank page.

"But I'm just gonna talk about the first part of it. That is what I think he feels I'd be most helpful with. Because that was my biggest lesson to learn... that our evolution as leaders is demonstrated by what we choose to focus on."

Jenn was leaning forward, ready to write what came next.

Roberto took a quick swig of his coffee. *"So, the first thing most leaders focus on is STUFF. And that is exactly what I did when I first transitioned from being a teacher to an administrator. Stuff is easy. Stuff is comfortable. A perfectly organized spreadsheet doesn't judge you or ask difficult questions that you can't answer yet, unlike... well, you know."*

He gestured subtly towards the people around them. He looked up to see if she was understanding. *"You, uh, have any idea what I mean?"*

Jenn nodded without looking up from the page. *"Of course..."*

"Okay. So, two years ago, I was good at my job as a teacher. I knew my stuff. But when I moved into a role where I was responsible for serving, supporting, caring about, and developing people, I focused on stuff... and that hurt the teachers on my team."

Jenn looked up, confused. *"Hurt them? How?"*

"Well, I am not the most gregarious person on staff there. I kept to myself as a teacher for the most part... and that is the way I started out as an administrator. I stayed in my office, on my computer, like a hermit. I ordered the stuff we needed, and I checked off the daily things on my calendar. I handled student behavior issues and did the classroom teacher observations. The printers in the building were thriving, but I wasn't a good leader..."

Roberto was funny, and likeable. But Jenn wrinkled her eyebrows. Because it sounded like her last few weeks in her position. She was doing the job as it was defined officially... and then some, since she took on so much of her team's work to get projects across the finish line of milestone dates for production...

But she understood what he was describing. It was her.

"I needed to find ways to connect so they didn't resent my suggestions and support. I had to learn that people need good tools to help them in their jobs... pens that work, software that doesn't crash, and maybe a boss who remembers their names. But supplies and software are only as effective as the people who are using them."

Jenn thought about the updated reporting form that a few people on the team had not been completing correctly, that she had been forced to go back and correct. And the new copier she was so excited about, that somebody had jammed up because they loaded the ink cartridge the wrong way just two weeks ago.

"Dad explained to me that I was limiting my impact because I was limiting my focus to STUFF. And that if I wanted the stuff to be used more effectively - whether it was a piece of equipment or a piece of advice - then I needed to change my focus by giving more attention to my understanding of my STAFF..."

Tony surprised them both by setting a red Deja-Brew mug full of black coffee on the table beside Jenn's open notebook. *"Looks like you two have covered a lot already!"*

Roberto smiled and motioned for Tony to sit and join them again.

"We have. Roberto is remarkable," Jenn said.

As Tony took his seat, Roberto began to rise. He peeked at his left wrist to check his watch, grabbed the small chunk of remaining blueberry muffin from the table, and finished it as he stood. *"Gotta get to school. Fridays are always an adventure, like a rabid teenage zombie apocalypse."* He smiled and held up his right hand to Jenn. *"Really a pleasure to meet you. I hope what I shared will be helpful."*

Jenn smiled back and thanked him as he rushed off, then leaned back in her chair with the fresh mug of coffee cupped in both her hands. *"Your son is impressive, Tony. Thank you for inviting him."*

Tony scratched absently at the gray and black stubble on his chin. *"He is a good boy. A good man. The school is good for him, and he has grown into a very effective leader. Just as you will!"*

Tony pointed at her playfully. *"I know it may have felt unexpected for you, but he and I meet here every Friday morning at 6:30 to chat. He sees his sister, and we get to discuss whatever is on his mind about his work. And what he talked about, it is important for us to discuss further. He told you about the need for leaders to evolve in their focus, yes?"*

Jenn looked down at the page of notes she had taken. *"Yes. Exactly."*

"Good. Then we will add to the lesson to be sure you leave with a clear understanding of how to begin to shift from STUFF to STAFF. We will start with naming all four parts of the lesson..."

He reached over and motioned to take her pen, and with his other hand he twisted the notebook around to face him.

Jenn surrendered the pen and watched him draw another set of steps.

"The evolution of leaders is demonstrated by what they choose to focus on..."

Tony drew another familiar set of four lines. On the bottom, he wrote **STUFF**. Above that, he wrote the word **STAFF**. Then he wrote **SELF**.

And at the top of the steps, he wrote the word **SYSTEMS**.

"As Roberto explained, many leaders get stuck focusing on their circumstances, surroundings, and the materials they will use. And those things are important, of course, but they do not decide how successful your team is. Your husband, the basketball coach, would say they don't win you any games..."

"It is the people who you trust to use those tools and overcome those circumstances who are truly responsible for the wins you achieve as a leader. You depend on your people to use those things productively. And when you focus on your staff, they become more willing and prepared to use all your stuff more productively."

Tony remembered to give the pen back to her, and then Jenn began writing underneath the drawing he had made.

Now Tony tapped the table to emphasize his next point. *"And what you will get today, Jenn, are a few things that will help you connect with and develop your staff. We won't have time for the other two parts of the lesson, but those we can come back to next week. Sound okay?"*

Jenn answered quickly. *"Yep. I realize I've been doing a lot in the background to make sure our projects are on schedule, but I've not spent much time talking with the team at all the last few weeks. I've just been sending out instructions and focusing on stuff, like Roberto said..."*

She was curious to hear about the two things he had promised to share. She definitely needed to do a better job connecting with and improving her team.

"Okay, the first thing you will want to know if you are interested in having more influence with your team is that they need to trust you. And trust doesn't happen without intentional interactions that demonstrate you are trustworthy..."

Jenn frowned. *"Yeah, as good as I was as a designer, I don't think they fully trust me yet as a manager."*

"That makes sense. Trust isn't built overnight, Jenn. It's like a three-legged stool - things get wobbly if even one leg is weak."

"Three-legged stool, huh? Okay, I'm listening..."

Tony motioned to borrow her pen again. He talked as he drew a stool on the bottom of the next page in her notebook.

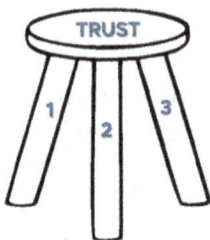

TRUST

1 - COMPETENCE

2 - CONCERN FOR OTHERS

3 - COMMITMENTS KEPT

"There are three things you need to demonstrate to strengthen trust with your coworkers or your clients, or anyone you care about. The first is COMPETENCE IN YOUR ROLE, the second is CONCERN FOR OTHERS, and the third is COMMITMENTS THAT YOU KEEP."

Jenn wondered if she had been good at any of the three.

Tony handed the pen back and continued to explain... *"First is competence. People trust you when they know you're good at what you do. If your team believes in your expertise, they'll feel more confident relying on you."*

Jenn mumbled, *"Not me yet..."*

"Exactly. Yet is a powerful word. Just keep learning. And don't be too upset about where you are today - you must be willing to be bad long enough to get better. And the truth is this first leg actually has the least impact on most relationships. People are willing to give you grace to grow if they are convinced you are dependable with the other two..."

Jenn perked up. *"Got it. So, explain the second leg?"*

"Concern for Others. If people think you only care about results, the relationship suffers. They need to feel valued as a person, not just for their performance. Does your husband only care

about his top scorer, or does he ask about and encourage the last person on the bench who is still developing?"

Jenn wrote as he spoke, nodding as she did.

"You demonstrate that with simple things, like listening to them and understanding their perspective, checking in on them, celebrating wins, and remembering small details about their lives, showing them that they matter to you."

Jenn held her pen motionless as she heard and considered Tony's list of the many things she had not been doing. *"And the third leg?"*

Tony shrugged as he spoke. *"Keeping Commitments. If you say you'll do something, follow through. It's about reliability. I believe that is your strongest leg right now, Jenn. I imagine people see you consistently keep your word. And that is a good thing for your team."*

"Guess I need to start strengthening the other two..."

"You will, Jenn. Awareness of the problem often leads to the solution."

Jenn put the pen down on the page. She made a fist to release the tightness out of her writing hand. Then she looked up with her eyes squinted, preparing to ask her question. *"So... so how? How do I do that? And with a hybrid team I don't get to see often... What is going to fix those other legs?"*

Tony smiling back annoyed her a bit. *"Do you remember what leadership is, Jenn?"*

That caught her by surprise. Yes. They had discussed that on their first day together. She flipped back to the front of her notebook and read through the ideas she had recorded from their conversation on Tuesday.

There it was. "Yes. You said leadership is the influence of our interactions."

Tony nodded. *"Good. So let me ask... how many interactions are you having with your people?"*

Jenn shrugged. *"I don't know. Not many, I guess..."*

"Exactly. And the ones you have been having, I would wager, have been more pointed than productive, yes?"

Jenn tilted her head. *"Yep. They have."*

"So, I believe both of your weaker legs would be strengthened if you focused on being more curious and considerate with your people. The second thing I wanted to show you will help with that..."

He reached over and spun the notebook around so he could write in it. *"Borrow your pen again?"*

Jen smirked at him and held it out for him to grab.

Tony excitedly took it, and at the top of the next blank page he wrote in large capital letters: 1 ON 1 CONVERSATION MAP FOR JENN.

Then he began to draw a lot of dashes all over the top half of the page. Jenn had no idea what he was doing. But the dashes made a winding path. And at the end of the path, Tony drew what she thought was supposed to be a treasure chest. Tony drew a big X beside it.

Then, before handing her the pen back, he wrote the numbers 1 through 4 at different places along the path he had drawn.

"That looks interesting..." Jenn said, curious to hear his explanation.

"No matter how many times I tried to make it more structured, the best one-on-one conversations always seem to meander. They aren't a straight line if you are really listening and being curious. But these conversations are the key to you building better relationships, developing trust, and growing the people on your team..."

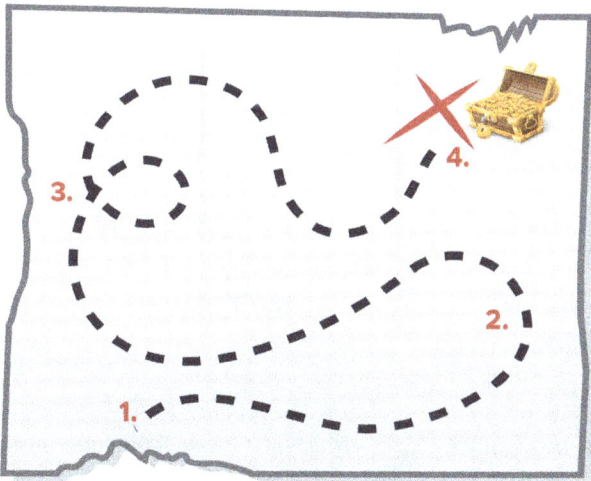

Tony pointed at the drawing and moved his finger around for emphasis. *"And don't think there isn't a path, even if it winds about a bit. Your job is to follow the path, and not get too worried if it meanders some."*

"And those 4 numbers are the things I need to get to if I want to reach the treasure?"

"That's it exactly. And the treasure is a better team that feels like you know and care about them. A team who trusts you!"

Jenn wrote the numbers 1–4 down the left side of the bottom of the page, where Tony had provided the unexpected artwork. *"Alright then. What are the four things that need to be part of the conversation?"*

Tony grinned at her. *"Glad you asked! But first, let me share what I've found helpful in scheduling your conversations. I think they are most effective if you meet once a week. At least once every two weeks. And they can be just thirty minutes long. But they are a powerful way to spend time with your team, and those interactions can become the foundation of your leadership.*

Jenn looked at him when she had finished writing those down in the margin.

"Good. The first part of the conversation is all about them. Focus on CONNECTION for the first third of your time together. For your first conversation, maybe start with something simple to get to know them, like 'tell me about your family...' or ask them 'what about this job really excites you?'

"Then in your weekly meetings, after that, you could open by asking 'What's on your mind?' or 'What's got you excited about this week?' Give them a chance to set the topic for that first part, and stay curious. Let this be when you learn more about their life outside work, their vacations, their hobbies.

"Number two is where you shift the conversation to their CHALLENGES. You can ask something like 'What's the biggest

challenge you're dealing with now?' This is where you invest time to help them identify obstacles they need to overcome.

"Number three is about CLARITY. And this part can be dangerous - because sometimes it will be easy to just tell them what you think they should do. You may have clarity and understanding of the situation, but it isn't about you. It's about helping them get clarity for themselves. It's about helping them grow in awareness and confidence.

"So you want to ask something like 'What do you see as possible solutions?' to get them to come up with ideas and options. And the last part of this step is to have them identify what might get in the way of their plans, so they are prepared for it..."

Tony paused here, as he realized that was a lot for Jenn to write.

Jenn finished recording his words on the page moments later, and looked up. "This *is very helpful, Tony. I would have never tried this without these guidelines to move me through what it should look like..."*

"Well, you will have to be bad long enough to get better. And it will feel awkward at first. But these conversations are a great tool to connect with and support your people.

"Okay, so the last part of the conversation map is their COMMITMENT about what they will do next. Ask them to explain it. Say something like, 'What specific action will you take before our next conversation, and how can I support you?'

"This is where the treasure is. The treasure at the end of each conversation is the connection and trust that you will create. But it is also the development of your people and making them

feel understood and supported. Because your success is not based on what you know... it is determined by what your people choose to do..."

Tony sat back in his chair and watched her pen move furiously across the page. When she stopped, he spoke again. *"We've covered a lot today, Jenn! Any thoughts about what you heard?"*

Jenn bit her lip and nodded. *"I need to schedule some conversations with my team. I need to build trust with them and be more curious..."*

"I'm glad to hear you want to do that. And we'll discuss the last two steps in the evolution of your focus on Tuesday, okay?"

Jenn smiled and closed the notebook.

"Self and systems next week then!"

She rubbed the palm of her right hand. *"Can't believe how sore my hand gets from all that writing..."*

Tony stood up, and she did the same. She slid the red notebook into her purse. He offered her his hand. *"I hope you have a pleasant weekend. I've got a team meeting this morning, and my grandson is coming over to stay with us. My wife and I are excited!"*

Jenn smiled. *"You too, Tony... I've actually got a ton of work to get through to catch us up on some projects. And I'll talk with Brian about those tickets!"*

CHAPTER 6

CURIOUS CONNECTIONS

Jenn had a busy weekend... The smell of new carpet filled her house.

It was installed Saturday afternoon, so there was no more reminder of the leak that had led her to meeting her unexpected mentor. She went with nearly the exact same color as what had been removed, and it looked terrific.

She had also been able to talk with Brian a couple of times. That always made things better. He seemed pleased that she had someone helping her with the challenges of her new role. It felt so good to hear his voice. She missed him. And she was excited to hear him say he would finally be returning home with the team on Thursday.

But as much as he seemed to be enjoying his role as part of a major program coaching staff, she could hear frustration in his voice. All he would say was that there were a few guys on the team he was still trying to connect with. But he assured her that the head coach was thrilled with his attention to detail and scouting.

That was good, she guessed.

When she hadn't been on the phone with Brian, or watching the carpet installers work, most of her time had been spent on her laptop. She wanted to make sure she had good news to share on her next call with Lewis. That meant checking on all the designs her team had been working on, and going over everything that would need to be submitted to the production team.

Her eyes were exhausted by Sunday afternoon from staring at her screen to check the measurements and drawings and each of the entries on the project forms. She didn't want there to be any mistakes.

By Sunday evening, she finally got around to sending out the emails that were last on her to-do list. She wanted to schedule those individual conversations Tony had mentioned. She needed to build better connections with her team. Dooley was nudging her elbow, ready for his evening potty break, when she pressed send on the last of her email invitations.

A bright moon was out when she finally got her shoes on to take him for the last walk of the day, much later than normal. Jenn enjoyed the crisp cool air and feel of fall coming soon. And for the first time in months, she felt excited about her upcoming week at work.

———

Tuesday morning, she was surprised to discover that she had arrived at Deja-Brew before Tony. It was just after 6:40 when she walked in, and when she didn't see him at any of the tables, she walked up to the counter to order her coffee. She got a muffin, too. Banana Nut. The teenager behind the register smiled excitedly as she served up both. Jenn carried the mug and the muffin over to where she and Tony had sat on Friday.

After removing the notebook from her purse and placing it on the table, she tore a piece from the top of the muffin off and took a bite, watching customers come in and leave for what was only a few minutes before Tony's familiar shape stepped through the door. He had on the same uniform she had always seen him wearing - a short-sleeve knit polo shirt with the Estrada Plumbing company logo, khaki pants, and faded white athletic shoes.

Framed by his gray and black stubbly cheeks, a warm smile emerged and greeted her. The wrinkles around his eyes grew deeper for a moment, and Jenn was glad to be here with him for another morning chat. *"Good morning, Jenn,"* he said. He took the seat across from her.

"Hello Tony. Looking forward to our time together today!" She opened the notebook and placed a pen on the next blank page. She had filled over twenty pages with notes from their first week together.

One of the employees came over in a blue Deja-Brew t-shirt to greet Tony at the table and ask what he would like before he could respond to Jenn. *"Dark roast again today, Mr. Estrada?"*

"Yes, thank you!" he replied.

Then, as she scurried away to fetch his order, Tony turned again to Jenn. *"So, how are things with you? Did you have a nice weekend?"*

Jenn nodded. *"I did. Got a lot done, actually. Talked with Brian. Played with Dooley. Got the new carpet installed. Spent a lot of time reviewing and correcting the project plans my team has been working on to be ready for when I talk with my boss again next week. And I reached out to everyone on the team to start scheduling the one-on-ones you talked about last Friday!"*

She raised her eyebrows and tilted her head proudly, then tore off another chunk of muffin top and popped it into her mouth for emphasis, awaiting his praise.

Tony nodded slowly. Before he spoke, the server brought his mug and placed it on the table. He smiled and waved his thanks to the waitress, and let the coffee cool. *"I'm so glad you are setting up the individual conversations with your team. Did you have any yesterday?"*

Jenn nodded again with pride, finishing her bite. *"I did! Two of them. And like you said, they were awkward at first. But I was honest about just wanting to get to know them better. And I asked the questions you suggested. I even printed them out on a piece of paper and took notes..."*

Tony listened without responding.

"And they went better than I expected. I mean, the first one was no problem, because I have known Tanya and she does good work, and we got along as teammates before. But it helped to hear what she was excited about and then what she was

challenged with. And then asking for her ideas on what she thought would be possible solutions. It was good."

Jenn's face lit up with excitement. "But the second *call was wild. I was honestly kind of dreading it, because Dan has been almost rude to me in his emails. He is older, and I thought he might just resent me being his manager or something - he's always done good work, but recently he just seemed off, you know?"*

Tony reached for his mug as she continued.

"But I had no idea what was going on. I just assumed he was upset with me, right? And I had no idea what he was dealing with, Tony. His wife has been sick. She's been going through chemo treatments for skin cancer. And I didn't know!"

At that, Tony's face changed. His usual objectively patient and curious turned clearly to pleased. *"I am proud of you, Jenn. That is a difficult conversation. But it sounds like it was helpful for both of you?"*

Jenn nodded. *"It really was! He has always kept kind of to himself. But yesterday I learned what's been on his mind. I think he was glad I asked about him. And knowing that will help me serve, support, and care about him better, right?"*

"Yes, Jenn. Right. My Tia used to say that sometimes the people we work with are like horses with a burr under their saddle. They are difficult to work with, not because they are bad, but because something is affecting them... Our job is to adjust how we interact to discover the burr in their saddle. When you find the burr, if you can remove it, the horse always runs better."

"I've got a couple of in-person conversations in the office scheduled for today, and the rest of the calls scheduled for tomorrow. We'll see if I find any burrs..."

Tony sat back in his chair and pointed at her proudly. *"One-on-ones stop small issues from growing into larger problems. They build connection and understanding, and they help us inspire growth and uncover aspirations that our people have... And they help us adjust ourselves to become the leader they need us to be."*

She took a sip of her coffee, then grabbed her pen, excited to get started. *"Like the wrench you always carry around in your pocket?"*

"You are a smart one!"

"Okay... so where were we?"

Tony chuckled. *"Why don't you tell me?"*

Jenn flipped back a few pages in the notebook to remind herself. *"The evolution of leaders. Your son talked about not being too distracted by focusing on stuff. Then you talked about the importance of focusing on my staff. You went through the three things that build or sabotage trust..."*

She flipped the page back to the next blank one. *"And we finished on Friday with the one-on-one conversation map. You said the treasure was a better team that feels like I know and cared about them."*

Still leaning over, she looked up at him, ready for him to take the reins of the conversation and begin teaching.

"Let's stay there for a bit longer, focusing on your staff, Jenn. Having regular one-on-one interactions and building trust with your people are very important. You need to focus on strengthening those connections so that when you need to share corrections, it still feels like support and service, not assault..."

Tony watched her write. *"You want to build relationships strong enough to support the weight of an uncomfortable truth when you need to share it. And it's not just about your connection with your team, but also about their connection to each other. So, today I'll help you connect your staff to each other. And I'll share how to correct them effectively when you need to. Sound good?"*

Jenn nodded.

"Good. So today we will talk about PROFITABLE FLUFF and POINTING AT PROBLEMS. The first is important if you want to be good at the second."

Now Jenn was the one who was chuckling. *"Okay, I'll bite. What is profitable fluff?"*

Tony sat up a bit straighter to explain. *"Have you heard of team building, Jenn?"*

Jenn rolled her eyes a bit. *"Sure. But I don't think that stuff works... Do you?"*

"No and yes. I wasn't a fan. Still not a fan of much of it. I think some activities organizations invest in are more recreational and really just fluff..."

Jenn nodded, relieved Tony wasn't going to encourage her to take her team bowling or out for happy hour drinks. Nothing he had shared up to this point suggested he would be comfortable holding hands or singing songs with his plumbing employees. His teaching so far had been pretty practical and helpful.

"But," Tony said, holding up a finger, "I believe intentional team building is very important and PROFITABLE FLUFF. Leaders need to design opportunities for their people to connect and increase their awareness of themselves and other team members...

"Personality styles and conversations around values and personal experiences help build trust and familiarity among your team - and improve the chances they will talk to each other and collaborate when they have questions or challenges."

Jenn wasn't yet convinced. "Really, Tony? You think so?"

"I do. Completely. You think you can depend on accidental connections driving collaboration and making people more comfortable sharing their mistakes or needs with each other? Not gonna happen..."

He shook his head for emphasis. "An effective leader has to schedule and engineer experiences to help those things happen. And the best team building experiences end up being your most valuable leadership development training. If it's done well, intentional team building becomes profitable because it improves communication and productivity. But it starts with connection. Let me ask you this..."

Jenn stopped writing in her notebook and looked up to meet his eyes for the question he had promised.

"Would knowing more about your team help you lead them better?"

Jenn nodded quietly.

"And would it help their coworkers work with them better?"

Jenn nodded reluctantly again.

"So, when will you and your team learn this information?" Tony paused to let her process the question and reach the conclusion he desired. *"Wouldn't it be helpful if you could provide opportunities for your team to learn about each-other's family situations, favorite activities and things, flaws and skills, and future plans? If you had operating instructions that helped you understand their preferences and personalities?"*

Jenn signed, realizing the accuracy of his words. *"Okay. But what would that look like? I don't want to play laser tag."*

Tony laughed. *"You schedule it. Just like your one-on-ones. Just like weekly team meetings. Intentional team building is something you put on the calendar every few months. And it's not about just going to an escape room together... it's about facilitating transformative experiences that shift the awareness of your people. That is what improves behaviors and affects your bottom line."*

Jen stopped writing and pulled the paper liner from the bottom of her muffin, tearing off a piece to chew on as her mind churned.

Tony waited patiently for her to respond to his last comments.

Jenn swallowed her bite and pressed her lips together. *"I guess I get it. I need to do something to improve how our team collaborates, and maybe that would help. So, what's the last thing for focusing on my staff, then?"*

Tony pointed at her notebook. *"Write this at the top of your next page. Ready?"*

Jenn nodded, pen in hand again.

"POINT AT PROBLEMS, NOT PEOPLE"

She wrote it large across the top of the page.

Tony started to explain. *"The challenge I had with addressing problems as a young leader was that people would get defensive and upset. They felt I was pointing at them. And that wasn't helpful. Remember when I said to build relationships strong enough to support the weight of uncomfortable truths? That is why team building and one-on-ones are valuable. If people know you care about and want the best for them, it is much easier to make conversations about pointing together at a problem that together you can commit to finding a solution for...*

"But having those uncomfortable conversations is part of your role as a leader... your team expects you to be the guardrails that keep people on the road of acceptable and productive behaviors... and it is an opportunity to develop yourself and your team by showing compassion and seeking solutions creatively. Our job as leaders is to POINT at the problem, and support the person!"

Jenn stopped writing and looked up. *"That sounds a lot easier than it is."*

"That is why I want to share a template for you to use when you need to prepare for one of those conversations. It uses the word POINT as an acronym..."

Tony held out his hand to ask for her pen, and she placed it in his palm. She took the initiative to turn the notebook to where it was in front of him. He nodded his thanks. Then he proceeded to write those five letters down the left side of the page.

Tony gave back the pen so Jenn could record his explanation. *"Jenn, effective leaders "POINT" at an issue or unproductive behavior while still appreciating and encouraging the person... and each letter of the acronym is important if you want the interaction to affect behaviors without hurting feelings. The first letter, P, is for PERMISSION AND PURPOSE. Of course, you will need to meet individually with them. Then share that you have noticed something that could help them accomplish a goal they feel is important, and then ask if it's okay to share the idea."*

"I ask for permission first?"

Tony grinned. *"Exactly. It's like opening the door for a conversation instead of barging in."*

Tony pointed down at the page, beneath where she had been writing. *"Next, the O is for OBJECTIVELY DESCRIBING THE OBSERVED BEHAVIOR. Second, share factual descriptions of their behavior. It is important to be as specific as possible and to the point. DON'T waste time dancing around the issue... just give them the numbers or observed behavior that needs to be addressed."*

"Okay, so... facts only?" Jenn asked, without looking up.

"Exactly. No opinions, no emotions. Just describe what you saw or what the data shows. Be specific and direct—no dancing around the issue.

"Next, the I is where you IDENTIFY THE IMPACT ON THE TEAM. This is where you build empathy. Help them see how their behavior impacted a teammate, a client, or the overall team. And this can be either positive or negative."

Jenn sat up and paused. *"That makes sense... If they understand the bigger picture, they're more likely to see the need to change."*

"Yes, empathy is the foundation of accountability. Now, N stands for NEGOTIATE NEXT STEPS. Instead of telling them what to do, ask for their ideas on how to improve. Get their input on what needs to happen to move forward. When they're part of the solution, they're much more likely to own it."

Jenn nodded as she wrote.

Tony finished the explanation of his acronym. *"And the last letter, T, is to TRACK THEIR PROGRESS."*

Jenn was still leaning over the notebook, but tilted her head to look over at him. *"Follow up?"*

"Yes, good. Set a date to circle back and check on their progress. This is where you reinforce positive changes or adjust the plan if needed."

He pointed at the page of notes she had been taking. *"And when they make progress, acknowledge it. A simple 'thank you' goes a long way."*

Jenn looked at what she had written, considering each part of the process.

THE "POINT" FEEDBACK MODEL

P = PREPARE WITH PERMISSION & PURPOSE

O = OBJECTIVELY DESCRIBE THE BEHAVIOR

I = IDENTIFY THE IMPACT ON TEAM

N = NEGOTIATE NEXT STEPS

T = TRACK THEIR PROGRESS

"That all makes sense. But..." She paused, a bit hesitant. *"That's a lot to remember in the heat of the moment."*

Tony nodded, agreeing with her. *"That's why it is important to prepare for what you want to say before you are in the middle of a conversation where you need to say it well. And it will help you if you practice using the model with positive comments first."*

Jenn raised her eyebrow at him. *"Positives?"*

"Absolutely. Before you use it to address a problem, spend your first two weeks using it to point out and acknowledge positive behaviors. It's a great way to build up your people while you get comfortable with the process."

Jenn sat up, popping the last bit of muffin into her mouth. A smile spread across her face as she chewed. *"I like that. Reinforce the good stuff... and then we'll both be ready for the tougher conversations when they need to happen."*

Tony grinned and lifted his mug. *"Now you've got it. Cheers to you, Jenn!"*

She held up her mug in reply to his cheers, and they both finished their coffee.

Tony set his mug on the table and looked at his watch. *"That's it for today, I think. You're going into the office, right?"*

"Yep, every Tuesday."

"Well, good luck with the one-on-ones you have scheduled. Tomorrow we'll look at the next step up in your evolution of focus... sound good?"

Jenn stood up. *"Very good, Tony. Thank you."*

"My pleasure, Jenn. I'm truly glad to help. And I've got another meeting of my own to get to... so have a wonderful day. I'll see you here in the morning. And I'll bring you something I think you'll find useful to improve your awareness of your staff!"

He turned to leave. Jenn again noticed the wrench peeking out of his back pocket. She collected her things and followed behind him a few moments later, wondering what he was planning to give her. Then she turned her thoughts to her team, and to the meetings and conversations she had ahead of her.

This could be a very productive day.

CHAPTER 7

POINTING FINGERS

When Jenn sat down across from Tony on Wednesday morning in the Deja-Brew coffee shop, there was a sheet of paper waiting for her on the table.

Before she examined it more closely, she turned her eyes to him. *"I've really enjoyed our mornings together, Tony. And I just needed to tell you that, as soon as I got the POINT model in my head yesterday, I wanted to use it immediately to address some issues I've been having with my team. But I didn't, because I heard your voice reminding me to acknowledge positive behaviors first..."*

She put her purse down on the floor and took the notebook out with one hand, fishing through it to find her pen with the other. *"That was a much more difficult task than I anticipated!"*

Tony grinned in understanding of her struggle. *"We see what we look for. Sometimes adjusting our lenses to change our focus takes a few days. A story from my Tia helped me with that as well."*

He waited for her to look up with curiosity. *"The times I would complain about problems my employees had created, she always reminded me of the same verse from the Bible. Proverbs 14:4. You might want to write this one down, Jenn..."*

He waited for her to open the notebook and click open the pen. *"Ready?"*

She nodded, smiling with eager anticipation.

"Good. Here it is. 'Where there are no oxen, the stable is clean. But you need oxen for a large harvest.' She knew I needed to hear that people are messy. But without them, you don't get things done that are bigger than you."

Tony smiled warmly at her.

When she finished writing down his wisdom, he pointed to the paper he had left for her to find when she arrived. *"That paper will help you understand your oxen. The more you know about your team, the better you can adjust to their needs to help them succeed.*

"I'll go fetch you a coffee while you take a moment to read over it. Should be pretty easy to understand. I use it with everyone on my team. We call it our TEAM MEMBER OPERATING INSTRUCTIONS. Helps me and my people be better with each other."

Tony got up to get Jenn a coffee. *"Want a muffin too?"*

Jenn shook her head as she picked up the paper and began to read.

It was a set of twelve questions for people to answer.

TEAM MEMBER OPERATING INSTRUCTIONS

Name _____   Birthday ___/___/_____

1 - What are 2 of your strengths as a team member?

2 - What are your preferred times for team communication?

3- What is the best way to contact you during the day?

4 – What is the most effective way to give you feedback?

5 – How do you prefer to be recognized for doing great work?

6 – What is something the team should know about you that has sometimes been misunderstood by your previous coworkers?

7 – What is something you need that you're not getting enough of?

8 – What is something you struggle with at times?

9 - What is your favorite snack food and candy?

10 – What is a pet peeve of yours that the team should know about?

11 – What is something someone could do to make your day better?

12 – Why are you excited about being part of this team?

Tony walked back over from the counter with a yellow mug in each hand, and placed one on the table in front of Jenn, before sitting down across from her. *"What do you think?"* he asked.

He sipped his coffee.

"I like it. Can I keep this?"

Tony nodded and waved his palm at her. *"Of course."*

Jenn folded it and placed it between the pages inside the notebook. Then she looked at him, ready to begin the day's lesson. Her notebook was open to the next blank page. At the top, she wrote the date. August 25th.

"Good. Today we shift our focus again," Tony said.

"We have gone from stuff to staff, and now we will go from staff to self. Focusing on staff is about improving your awareness of your people, and their awareness of each other. Focusing on yourself is about improving your own awareness of how you are leading and the impact you are having on your team's success. When you get better, the effectiveness of your staff and your stuff get better as well..."

He took a larger sip this time. *"And a powerful question you might want to write down to revisit and help take ownership of your influence is this..."* He paused to be sure she was ready.

Jenn peeked up, pen still poised above the paper, ready to record his words.

"What part of my leadership led to that result?"

Tony waited for her to write it down. *"Underline that one,"* he said.

She did.

"Focusing on yourself is about realizing you need to be an adjustable wrench. It is the most useful tool in the world, and the most valuable."

He reached in his back pocket and held up the one he kept there. *"Because it reminds you that you need to adjust to others if you want to change things."*

He shook the wrench in the air for effect, then returned it to his back pocket. *"Wishing others were something else that you expect them to be is frustrating for both you and them. Your job as a leader is to adjust to others - don't complain about their differences or imperfections. People aren't perfect. They are gonna always dirty up the manger like oxen. Focusing on yourself allows you to adjust how you interact with them so they can be productive."*

Jenn turned the page and continued to write, clearly adding a few of her own thoughts to what Tony had just shared. *"Okay - I hear you."*

Jenn put down her pen and focused on her own coffee for the next moment, thinking while she drank it. *"So..."* she put her mug back down on the table. *"You gonna tell me how to improve my awareness so I can be a better wrench?"*

She flashed a playful grin.

"I will share the first part. My daughter will stop by soon to talk with you about the other two parts of the lesson today. I asked her to join us for this topic specifically, because it nearly caused her to lose this business."

Tony looked around at the walls of the coffee shop, and his expression became vacant, as if he was remembering moments from the past. When his eyes returned to their table, he collected himself. *"Lucia can talk with you about her path, but I would like to start by telling you what made a huge difference for me in growing myself."*

Jenn nodded, still surprised to hear that Tony would not be the one delivering today's entire lesson.

Tony started sharing before she had the pen in her hand again. *"The habit I picked up that really helped me improve myself, the one I wish I had started earlier, is taking a few minutes at the end of each day to reflect. And I know it sounds like a simple thing, but it completely changes the way you lead. When you give yourself time to think back on your day, you start to notice patterns. You learn from mistakes, and start to really understand how your actions impact the people around you.*

"Reflection helps you learn from whatever happens. Every day. So, you get better at recognizing what's working... and what you want to do differently. And you start making adjustments that help you lead more effectively."

He pointed at the page to emphasize recording the next part. *"I have two simple routines - one in the morning and one in the evening. It doesn't take much time, and it's made a huge difference. You ready?"*

Jenn pointed at him with her pen to acknowledge she was.

"Good. So, in the morning, I take five minutes to prepare for the day. I go through a few quick questions that help me stay focused and intentional:

- *What's one thing I'm grateful for today?*
- *What's something I'm excited about?*
- *What's the thing I want to avoid?*
- *What's the thing I absolutely need to get done today?*

"Answering these each morning keeps me intentional about how I show up for my team, and helps me have more productive interactions. Then, at the end of the day, I set aside ten minutes for a different set of questions..."

Tony paused and grinned, tapping his temple with his index finger. *"This is the part where my real learning usually happens. I ask myself:"*

- *What were my two biggest wins or insights?*
- *What didn't go as well as I'd hoped, and how can I improve?*
- *Who did I connect with, encourage, or praise today?*
- *What's on the agenda for tomorrow?*

"Those reflection questions will help you if you use them. The more consistent I've been with it, the more I've seen myself and my team grow."

He waited to be sure she had written each of the questions down in her notebook. Then he pointed down at the page as he continued. *"And just like taking notes to remember important ideas, you will want to write down your answers to the question in a journal. Writing is the refining part of thinking. It helps you prioritize and polish thoughts so they are clearer to you."*

Tony sat back in his chair, and crossed his arms in front of his chest.

Jenn dropped the pen onto the notebook and grabbed her mug, still leaning forward as she drank the last of the coffee from it. The mug was still in her hand as she looked down and read the questions she had just added in her notes. *"Thank you, Tony."*

He closed his eyes and nodded as a reply. Then he leaned forward, moving his finger in a circular motion and pointing at the page she had filled with her notes. *"Try them out for a week. Go through the questions each day. I think you'll be surprised by how quickly it improves your awareness. But today's lesson is not over yet for you, my dear. You have the pleasure of talking with my daughter still ahead of you..."*

He turned his eyes to the counter, looking for his daughter.

Jenn followed his gaze and saw her wave to him as he beckoned her over with a thumb up in the air as his signal it was time for her portion of the program.

As Lucia approached, Tony lifted himself out of the chair to give her a hug. Lucia was in a green Deja-Brew t-shirt and jeans, and her black hair was pulled into a high ponytail today.

After kissing his daughter on the cheek, he looked back at Jenn, who was still seated. *"I'm going to leave you two ladies to chat with each other."*

He turned his body to allow Lucia space to take the seat he had vacated. *"Lucia, take good care of her for me... and thank you for agreeing to this today. I'm off to the office for a conversation with one of my plumbers!"*

Lucia smiled at him and waved as he walked away.

But instead of joining Jenn by sitting in the chair her father had just left open for her, she reached down and grabbed the two empty mugs. *"Let's not do this here,"* she said, a dimple showing as she grinned. *"Follow me."*

CHAPTER 8

DIFFERENT LENSES

Jenn grabbed her purse and notebook and got up. She hurried to follow Lucia, who was already moving briskly toward the back counter, which held a register and a display case for the muffins and other assorted breakfast pastries they offered.

On the side wall, nearest where customers placed their order, were logoed travel mugs of various colors and an assortment of bags of their ground coffee. Behind the counter stood three cheerful employees. Each one wore a different color company t-shirt, and were all busily focused on ringing up or preparing drinks for the current customers.

None of the three looked surprised when Lucia walked through the open space at the end of the counter, near the wall opposite the register, and motioned for Jenn to follow her to the back of the store.

Jenn watched the employees working as she apprehensively trailed Lucia.

The girl at the register smiled at her. Jenn returned her smile, and continued after Lucia, turning a corner and disappearing behind the wall of sinks and commercial coffee and latte machines and refrigerators.

Jenn walked through a hallway with shelves loaded full of all kinds of supplies, and watched as Lucia opened a door to what had to be her office.

Lucia sat down behind a dark-stained wooden desk, and motioned Jenn to sit in one of the two armless leather chairs in front of it. The L-shaped desk had pictures of Lucia and her family - a couple of small framed images of what must be her son, a larger gold frame of her with the boy and what must be his father, and an 8x12 white frame with a large family together inside the building before it had been completely remodeled.

Lucia peeked at a laptop screen open on the desktop beside the wall, then turned to Jenn with a curious look. *"I need your help, Jenn. I'm trying really hard to get better as a leader and business owner, and I'd like your advice..."*

Lucia looked across the desk intently at her. *"So, what is one thing I could do differently that would make this place better?"*

She waited for Jenn to think on it, eyes wide with interest to hear whatever Jenn was going to share as a possible opportunity to improve.

Jenn was searching her mind for what to say. She had only been here a few times, right? She didn't know what Lucia was like as a leader. She knew the coffee was good, and the service had always been pleasant and friendly. *"I, uh... everything really seems nice as it is."*

Lucia waited.

Jenn shrugged. *"Maybe post your Wi-Fi password at each table instead of just up at the counter?"* She said it like it was a question.

Lucia smiled. Her body relaxed from serious and intense to warm and comfortable. *"That's what I wanted to talk to you about today, Jenn. Because not doing THAT is what nearly cost me the coffee shop early on!"*

Jenn was confused.

Lucia realized the miscommunication and shook her head. *"Oh, sorry - not the Wi-Fi. Although that is a good idea. But I wanted to talk with you about getting feedback. That is the thing I wasn't doing as a leader that led to a couple of good employees leaving."*

Jenn sighed her understanding, and took out the notebook and her pen.

Lucia pointed at one of the picture frames. *"My son Nicolas is excited to go to a real college basketball game. Thank you for offering to do that, by the way..."*

"Oh, goodness. It's the least I can do after how nice your dad has been in meeting with me to talk about this stuff."

Lucia smiled. *"...and staff... and now self?"*

Jenn chuckled. *"Yes. Exactly."*

There was a pause. Jenn asked, *"Does he... does he do this with lots of people?"*

Lucia shrugged. *"Not really. Maybe once every few months. He'll meet someone he likes who he wants to help. And because I know how helpful the lessons were to me, and to those others, I'm happy to do this part of it."*

She grinned. "And it *doesn't hurt that we sell a few extra cups of coffee..."*

Jenn laughed with her.

"But you are here so I can talk about asking for advice." Lucia said. She reached into one of the drawers in her desk and pulled out a spiral notebook. It was worn from years of use, nearly falling apart. The blue cover was faded and creased in a few places. *"This was mine, by the way..."*

She flipped through it with her thumb, careful not to let any of the pages fall out. Then she slid it back into the drawer and sat straighter in her chair. She pointed at Jenn's notebook. *"Let's make sure I give you some helpful things to write down."*

Jenn opened it to the next blank page and nodded. *"Okay... ready!"*

"So, when dad first helped me buy this place, I felt this huge pressure, you know... I wanted it to succeed so badly. And I didn't realize I made it miserable for my team. You like movies, Jenn?"

Jenn nodded, curious where this was going.

"I love mysteries and thrillers... And the thing is, most of those movies, even though the audience might know who is responsible, is a lot of frustration with the hero trying to figure out who is responsible for the killing and damage that required their attention. That is what happens with most leaders in an organization. We are always trying to identify the villain... to look behind the symptom to find the problems that are keeping our teams from being successful. But what if the hero could see what the audience was seeing?"

She waited for Jenn to consider this. *"Dad was gonna talk with you earlier this morning about reflection, right?"*

Jenn glanced up and nodded.

"And that is helpful, don't get me wrong. But as a new business owner, no matter how much I reflected, I only came up with answers based on what I was seeing and the assumptions I was making. That's what led to two of my first set of employees leaving."

Lucia shook her head, still bothered by the memory. *"That is why I wanted to talk with you about Feedback. It is the second way to focus on growing yourself. And it gives you some different and very helpful answers to the question - 'What part of my leadership led to that result?'"*

Jenn was writing still.

And Lucia scooted her chair up so she was closer to the desk and leaned over it. *"Now, I don't think you are nearly as bad as I was about being stubborn or arrogant and refusing to ask other people for their perspectives. But I know my team suffered because I was more protective of my EGO than I was of them. I mean, I would give feedback to correct the flaws I saw* in others, but I never asked for feedback to address the flaws in myself."

She pointed at her chest when she mentioned her ego, and pointed out at the coffee shop through the wall of her office when she mentioned her employees. *"Effective leaders have to get past their EGO - and it took me longer than I'd like to admit to realize that. Now I say EGO is an acronym. It Eliminates Growth Opportunities! I mean, when you ask people if their boss or their teammates have blind spots, they say yes, of course they do - but when you ask most people if they have any blind spots, they don't want to admit them. Because we convince ourselves that we are not the problem, right?"*

She looked to Jenn for agreement. *"But, newsflash, when you really focus on improving yourself, you realize that in many ways you are the problem. And you start asking for help to fix what you need to fix. Cause, I mean, you don't know what your people are seeing unless you are curious and compassionate enough to get their perspective."*

"So the hero can see what the audience does?" Jenn inserted, playfully.

"Right!"

"And adjust yourself to what the team needs?"

"Exactly. You got this, Jenn! I mean, reflection is powerful. But sometimes we can't see things that are affecting the people we depend on. We need different perspectives to give ourselves a clearer picture of reality. For me, it was negativity and criticism that I didn't realize was discouraging my team. And asking for feedback is the shortcut that helps the hero

identify the villains and keep them from doing more damage..."

Lucia took a deep breath, and sighed.

"I mean, I had to learn that the best leaders aren't the ones with all the answers. They're the ones who ask better questions. And asking for feedback from your team is one of the fastest ways to grow as a leader. They'll tell you where you're doing well and where you might be missing something. But only if you ask...

And to get feedback, don't ask for feedback - ask for advice... It can feel a little uncomfortable at first, asking people to tell you what you could be doing better. But trust me, Jenn, the leaders who ask for feedback—"

Lucia corrected herself. *"Sorry, advice. They are the ones who grow the fastest. And to do it in a way that feels natural and actually gets you useful information, I have a simple five-step process that's worked for me."*

Jenn turned the page and waited for Lucia to share the five steps.

Lucia held up her index finger as she spoke again. *"Okay, so number one is CHOOSE THE RIGHT PEOPLE. Start by asking the people whose opinions you really respect - those who aren't just friends, but who will be honest with you. You want thoughtful people who've worked with you long enough to give meaningful feedback. Their perspective is gold because they've seen how you handle different situations over time..."*

Lucia held up two fingers now. *"Number two is ASK FOR THEIR HELP TO GET BETTER. Let them see a little vulnerability. Let them know you're committed to improving and value their perspective. Say something like I did when we first sat down, right? People are more willing to give helpful insights when they know you're genuinely trying to improve."*

Lucia waited for Jenn to finish writing before she continued on. *"Okay, number three is SHARE ONE SPECIFIC QUESTION. Don't ask more than one thing. And if you ask a vague question, you'll only get a vague answer. So, instead of asking, 'How am I doing?', ask something like 'What's one thing I'm doing that's been hurting the team?' And if they mention something, don't be afraid to ask for an example. It helps you get a clearer picture of what they're talking about.*

"Then number 4 is TAKE NOTES AND BE GRATEFUL. This part is huge. Write down what they say on a piece of paper or an index card. Don't trust your memory. And most importantly, listen without getting defensive. It's easy to want to explain or justify, but this is your chance to learn. Just take it all in and say thank you. Sincerely. Let them know you appreciate their time and honesty."

Lucia turned in her chair to peek at her laptop again, before she finished her list of steps.

Jenn couldn't see what was on the screen. She was busy writing.

After a short pause, Lucia refocused and turned back to face Jenn. *"And number five is FOLLOW UP WITH WHAT YOU DID. This step is where trust is built. Go back later and let them know what you've done with their advice. You don't have to implement everything, but showing that you've considered their input makes them feel valued and reinforces that their ideas matter. It might be as simple as saying, 'Hey, I've been working on what we talked about, and I've been trying to do X differently. Thanks again for your insights.'*

"*The question I asked you is a good one to start with. 'What's one thing I could do differently to make this a better place for you?' That question helps you figure out what your team needs. Because if you fail to see what is obvious to others, that becomes a problem. And over time, asking for advice creates a culture where people feel safe being honest, and that's where real growth happens - for everybody! Effective leaders stay coachable, and are greedy and grateful for the opportunity to see their impact through different lenses...*"

Lucia looked at her watch, and Jenn did the same. It was nearly 8:30.

Jenn needed to get into the office. She had a few more one-on-ones today, and needed to check in with the production team about two of their projects.

"Jenn, if you start doing this consistently, I promise you'll see a noticeable difference in how your team responds and how quickly you grow as a leader. And when you do, I'd love to hear what insights you're uncovering!"

Lucia stood up. "*Sorry, I've got a coaching call at 8:30. I hope this has been helpful for you?*"

Jenn closed her notebook and stood up as well. "*Very helpful. Thanks for your time, Lucia. I should get going too. I've got a few meetings I need to prepare for at the office today.*"

Jenn hesitated before leaving, though. "*You, uh. You have a coach?*"

Lucia nodded. *"I mean, yeah. I've hired a few coaches over the last year or so to help with different parts of my business. I think everybody needs a coach if they want to get the most out of themselves and their team."*

Jenn nodded, filing away the idea.

Lucia shrugged. *"I mean, just like you, my dad's questions and encouragement are what got me started with appreciating the value of reflection and feedback. But coaching is about someone else asking different questions that you wouldn't think of in reflection. And it's good to have an outside perspective and a little accountability to help you grow yourself faster than you could have without them."*

Lucia sat back down, and turned to her laptop. Clicking her mouse to open a window on the screen, she called out as Jenn opened her office door to leave. *"Please thank your husband for trying to get us seats at one of his games!"*

Jenn nodded. *"I will..."*

And she immediately began thinking about what was waiting for her in the office.

EFFECTIVE
— LEADERS —

CHAPTER 9

BETTER SYSTEMS

"Wow. Deja Brew all over again..." Jenn joked, as she sat down.

Tony had been at the table when she arrived. *"Happy Wednesday, Jenn!"*

He had a couple of papers on the table in front of him, turned face down so she couldn't see what was on them. He also already had a coffee mug in his hand.

She joined him, and now did what had become a habit - took out the red spiral notebook and a pen from her purse and placed them on the table in front of herself.

Before she could ask about them, Tony turned the first paper over and slid it to her. *"Put that inside your notebook. You can copy it down later in your own handwriting if you like, but I thought it would be a nice reminder from yesterday about how to improve yourself..."*

Jenn looked down at the paper. It had been printed out neatly for her. *"Not wasting any time getting into it today, huh?"* she poked.

Tony grinned, and the wrinkles at his eyes creased deeper as he nodded. *"The questions you ask are your greatest tool for improving yourself. Reflection questions you ask yourself. Feedback questions you ask your team. And coaching questions you hire somebody to ask you. This is a nice summary for you."*

IMPROVE YOURSELF BY IMPROVING YOUR QUESTIONS

"WHY...?" USUALLY LOOKS BACK TO CRITICIZE

"WHAT...?" & "HOW...?" LOOK AHEAD TO SOLUTIONS

EXAMPLE REFLECTION QUESTIONS: (you ask yourself)

- HOW CAN I BETTER HELP MY PEOPLE ACHIEVE THEIR GOALS?
- WHAT PART OF MY LEADERSHIP LED TO THAT RESULT?
- WHAT MIGHT BE GOING ON FROM THEIR PERSPECTIVE?

EXAMPLE FEEDBACK QUESTIONS: (you ask others)

- WHAT 2 THINGS SHOULD I KNOW ABOUT YOU TO LEAD YOU BETTER?
- HOW HAS MY LEADERSHIP MADE THINGS MORE DIFFICULT FOR US?
- WHAT SMALL HABIT COULD I CHANGE TO BE A BETTER LEADER?

EXAMPLE COACHING QUESTIONS: (others ask you)

- WHAT IS THE ONE ACTIVITY THAT WOULD HAVE THE MOST POSITIVE IMPACT ON YOUR PRODUCTIVITY OR RESULTS?
- HOW MUCH TIME ARE YOU SPENDING ON THAT ACTIVITY EACH DAY? (AND HOW MUCH TIME SHOULD YOU BE SPENDING EACH DAY?)
- WHAT WOULD YOU NEED TO BELIEVE TO COMMIT TO DOING IT?

Jenn focused for a moment on the top of the page.

"We didn't talk about this when I introduced the idea of reflection, or one-on-one conversations, but how you start your questions affects their outcomes. I've found that asking WHY

questions has a tendency to lead to negative responses, and usually look backward to blame. Ever have somebody ask 'why did you do that?'"

Jenn frowned as she replied. *"Yep."*

She had asked herself that too many times to count.

"It usually doesn't feel good. And rarely solves anything. But WHAT and HOW questions usually look ahead to solutions. Those are the ones you want to focus on."

Jenn nodded and folded the paper in half, then slid it into the front of her notebook. *"Thank you, Tony. That is helpful."*

He patted the other paper that was still face down on the table. *"Good. And I think you'll enjoy what I want to talk about today as well."*

"Systems, right?"

"You've been paying attention!"

"I have!" She smiled, proud of herself for remembering the next part of the evolution of leaders he had described, and curious to hear today's lesson.

She was startled by a person coming up behind her. It was Lucia, carrying a blueberry muffin and a large mug of fresh hot coffee. *"These are for you!"*

"Aw, thank you!" Jenn said.

She took the large green mug and sipped from it as Lucia placed the muffin and a few napkins on the table for her. *"Get you two anything else?"*

Jenn shook her head. Tony did the same.

"Okay then. I'll check on you later... And don't talk too fast, Papi!"

He smiled as Lucia walked back towards the register. *"I guess I should ask, Jenn. Anything happening with your team you'd like to talk about before we get started?"*

Jenn scrunched her lips together and looked away for a moment to consider. *"Well, as a matter of fact, I did finally talk with Maria yesterday, since we were in the office together. And that was interesting. But then our afternoon team meeting kind of got me frustrated again. It just didn't seem to go anywhere."*

Tony listened attentively. Jenn wasn't sure what he was thinking.

He processed her comment without expression. *"And what happened in your conversation with Maria? She is the one who had not been communicating much, correct? The one who didn't show up to a virtual meeting?"*

Jenn nodded. *"Right. And I wanted our first one-on-one to be in person, so yesterday was the first time I really talked with her..."*

"And what did you learn?" Tony asked.

She grabbed the muffin and took a small bite before continuing. *"Well, I learned Maria is the youngest person on the team. And it turns out she is pretty introverted. She's always been quiet in our meetings, I guess. But her work was terrific... just, not always on time. She just hadn't thought about how somebody might interpret her lack of communication..."*

"Like assuming she was lazy or irresponsible?"

Jenn nodded sheepishly. *"Yeah. Like that. And I didn't go into the POINT thing that you shared, because it was our first time really talking. I wanted to be sure she knew I cared about her and wanted to get to know her situation. But I think it will be good to use it if it happens again..."*

Tony smiled. *"I'm proud of you for that, Jenn. That was very wise. And you will find that her personal accountability will improve the more you help her connect with her team members and understand the larger goal she is contributing to. All accountability is driven by empathy - caring for how our actions affect somebody or something important to us."*

Jenn was pleased to hear him say that. *"Thanks, but then the team meeting had me all flustered again."*

"What happened there?"

"I don't know. I just ran through announcements and updates on the projects we have, but nobody seemed engaged or interested. They just sat there. I felt like it was a waste of time, really. I'm sure they did."

Tony patted the papers in front of him that were still face down. *"I think I can help with that,"* he said. Then he took a moment to enjoy the last of the coffee from his mug. He savored the taste, swallowed, and then refocused himself. *"Good, so we have talked about stuff and staff and self, and yes... today is about systems."*

Jenn turned to the next blank page in her notebook and held her pen ready.

"Think about systems this way... your house has systems that make things more comfortable and consistent. Like your electrical system to ensure you get power for all your devices with no surges or blackouts. Or your water system, to ensure you get fresh, clean water - hopefully with no clogs or leaks."

Jenn chuckled with him at that.

"If you didn't have those systems in place, you would worry about whether you could get consistent electricity or water. Stress is usually what you feel when you haven't built systems to create the quality and consistency you want in some area of your life. And as a leader, you want to define and document how to do the things your team needs to repeatedly do well. Because the reality is that the best intentions don't always translate into the best behaviors... and if you want people to do the right thing the right way at the right time, you need the right system in place to make it easy for them to do that..."

Jenn nodded as she wrote. *"Like pipes for water, right? All the pipes in my house, they are a system that helps the water flow where it is supposed to go..."*

"Good, Jenn. Yes. And following your analogy, when there is a problem with a system, that is when you see leaks happening and causing damage. So, your job is not just to create systems, but to update them when they need it. And virtually any process important to your team's performance can be documented as a system to help people do things better. Onboarding, client billing, checking inventory. The one-on-one conversation map I shared is just a system of what to ask and when..."

Jenn lifted her gaze from the notebook to Tony. *"But my team is different than your plumbers, and you have different systems than teachers or coffee shop owners? Right?"*

"Of course. But regardless of what your team needs to do more consistently, there are steps you can use to start building systems to help you and your team become more dependable. That is what I want to start with today..."

He held up what looked like an "okay" sign with his right hand. *"Three parts. Write one, two, three across your page, and I'll explain each step."*

She did.

"First, you need to PLAN it. What is the process you want to focus on, and what platform will you use to document it for quality and consistency? Get your team together, pick the process, then decide where it needs to live, whether that's a tool like Google Docs or somewhere else. The key questions for you in this step would be: What do we need to document, where will we keep it, and what does great look like?"

He waited for her to write that before he continued. *"Good, next, you need to PRODUCE it. Clearly documenting what needs to happen every time is important. Map out the steps, explain the 'why,' and add checkpoints or visuals to keep it simple. Make sure a new hire could follow it without a hitch. The key question for you in this step as the leader is: Are the steps listed clear and easy to follow?"*

"And third?" she asked.

"Well, last thing is you need to PERFECT it. Situations change over time. Check in annually or so to see if the process is still

relevant based on your goals and technology. Get your team's input to tweak the parts of it that need to be updated. And the key question for you in this step would be: Is this system still relevant and effective?"

1. PLAN	2. PRODUCE	3. PERFECT
Brainstrom platform and process to map out	Document your process with details	Evaluate occasionally to improve them

Jenn finished writing and grabbed her muffin. After taking a bite and chewing as she reviewed her notes, she spoke. *"I'm actually already thinking of a couple of processes we could take time to get clearer on. But what is the difference between a system and a habit, then?"*

Tony thought for a moment. *"Good question. I would say habits are behaviors that get repeated by one person, and systems are an organized process designed for a team to achieve quality results consistently by using those detailed routines.*

"Your husband is a coach, right? I'm sure he would tell you that all basketball teams set goals each season. But it is the quality of systems they create and follow that determine their results. That is true in business as well. And the three systems I want to

share before you leave today are for having clear daily priorities, for delegating successfully, and for having more effective meetings..."

"That sounds like a lot!" Jenn said. She flipped through her spiral notebook with her left hand. There weren't many blank pages left in the back of it.

"I think they will be helpful, especially after last weekend, Jenn. Do you recall telling me how you spent so much time reviewing and correcting stuff from your people? One thing I've learned is that your role as a leader isn't to take on your team's work. When you do, it can unintentionally take away their sense of ownership and limit their opportunities to learn and grow."

Ooh. That stung. Jenn felt like Tony was saying it compassionately. But he was right. She knew it hadn't been best for the team. It was something she had done herself, because she knew she would do it well. *"Wasn't expecting to hear that..."* she said.

"Things might get done faster in the short term if you take on more work yourself - but is your role to be efficient or effective in developing a more productive team?"

That may be true, but she was in no position to have Lewis upset about mistakes, so she had taken it on herself. *"Okay... then what do I do instead?"* Jenn was curious to hear his alternative, but her voice came out a bit edgier than she had intended.

Tony smiled warmly at her. *"Three things. A better to-do list, better delegation, and better meetings. Let's start with a better to-do list."*

He paused. *"So, a to do list is like..."* He pressed his lips together tightly, and his eyes went off to the side of the room. *"A to-do list is like a pile of books that you want to read. It is good to know what you intend to do, but difficult to carry the weight of them all throughout your day!"*

Tony pretended to cradle an invisible stack of books in his arms, moving his shoulders to emphasize the awkwardness of carrying a large stack of books.

She considered the metaphor he had created. *"Okay... don't carry too many books at the same time,"* she said wryly.

Tony grinned at her. *"That is not the system,"* he said. *"The system is to identify the next goal you are working to achieve, and then make a list of the important items that need to get done. Then on the left side of the page, you write the number 1– 5 beside the five tasks that you prioritize as most important. And you only focus on ONE TASK AT A TIME until you finish it! No more carrying too many books around with you all day!"*

He looked down at the papers still face down on the table in front of him. He turned over the next one and slid it toward her. *"It is the STARTING FIVE system for your daily to-do list... You can even begin the day with a list of more than five items. But your focus is on those top five priorities you numbered - and the others wait on the bench. They only get your attention if you complete the top five..."*

Jenn accepted the paper and looked it over. The concept was straightforward enough. List the top five priorities for the day, then rank them by importance. Still, she couldn't deny that staying focused had been a struggle lately.

My Starting Five

Date _____   Next Goal _____

Priority (#1-5)	Activity to Complete	Completed?
_____	_____	____
_____	_____	____
_____	_____	____
_____	_____	____
_____	_____	____
bench	_____	____
bench	_____	____
bench	_____	____
bench	_____	____
bench	_____	____
bench	_____	____
bench	_____	____

Work in twenty-minute sprints – and for any items you were unable to complete, simply relist, prioritize and rank the items on a new sheet each night to prepare for the following day!

She was constantly doing things that weren't really a priority, usually because they were more comfortable for her. Or because she got distracted with something else that drew her attention away from the task she was working on. "*Okay. I hear you, Tony. I do. But I get distracted sometimes. And then I do stuff lower on the list - or not even on it...*"

Tony nodded. "*That just makes you human. Let me tell you what I've found helpful. First, turn this thing on silent and put it somewhere it won't bother you."* He pulled a cell phone from his front pocket, showed it to her, and put it away. *"And just commit to a twenty-minute sprint. Work for twenty minutes at a time, uninterrupted. I think that is how long your husband's team plays in basketball... and just like they have a halftime break, you can take a break before another twenty-minute sprint. The key is that those twenty-minute work segments can only focus on the top five priorities you have for that day..."*

Jenn felt like she could do that, but she still wasn't sure the starting five system would really work for her. She always had a lot more than five things to do. *"Okay, and what about those days when there are a lot more than five things that need to get done, you know?"*

"I do. That is why I want to share the next system with you..."

He turned over the next sheet of paper and slid it to her. Jenn saw four phrases typed in blue, with questions underneath each heading. She looked over the steps, then up at Tony. "So, delegation is about TIME? I could definitely use more of that..."

Tony surprised her when he shook his head. *"Well, delegation is actually less about saving your TIME and more about investing your TIME in others. Remember, our main role as leaders is to serve, support, care about, and develop the people on our team. Poor leaders only delegate when they are drowning and desperate - and they treat delegated tasks like a wedding bouquet - they just throw it to someone blindly and don't follow up."*

He motioned with his hand, tossing an invisible bouquet behind him. *"But effective leaders see delegation like handing-off a baton in a relay race - careful it doesn't get dropped, so it keeps moving toward the finish line."*

THE TASK DELEGATION TEMPLATE

Follow this simple conversation structure to quickly prepare for delegation conversations with your team. It's a system designed to be completed in under ten minutes, helping you ensure clarity as you develop your people!

T.I.M.E. FOR DEVELOPING YOUR PEOPLE...

-TARGET THE IMPORTANT TASK:
THE TASK IS:

-IDENTIFY THE INDIVIDUAL:
I CHOSE YOU BECAUSE:

-MANDATE IMPORTANT METRICS
SHOULD BE COMPLETED BY:

WHAT GOOD LOOKS LIKE:

WHAT GREAT LOOKS LIKE:

-EQUIP WITH RESOURCES AND EVALUATE:
TOOLS YOU MAY FIND HELPFUL:

PEOPLE YOU MAY FIND HELPFUL:

OUR NEXT PROGRESS CHECK-IN WILL BE:

Jenn slid the paper into the front of her notebook with the others he had given her. There was still one paper left in front of Tony, and she was curious what it would focus on. But for now, she wanted to get the delegation process down. She wrote the first of the four phrases at the top of the next black page. *"Okay then, target the task. I'm ready for it..."*

Tony smiled at her impatience. *"Well, before we get to the process, I want to be sure you understand the why behind the how. Delegation is not about dumping undesirable things off your plate. It is for developing your team. People want to grow and add new skills. And leaders help them do that by delegating appropriate tasks to the right person with clear expectations and helpful support."*

Jenn wrote, but her face was scrunched up as she did. *"So, what is an appropriate task?"*

*"That is a good question, Jenn! Because if it is a critical task, you wouldn't hand it off to people who are unprepared to carry them to the finish line. The decision to delegate any task as a leader should be based on two things: the level of risk it presents to your organization, and the capability of the person on your team. So, to **Target Appropriate Tasks** for delegation, there are a few questions you'll want to ask yourself..."*

He looked over to see if she was ready to write them.

"Good. Okay, here they are..."

- *Is this a critical task that is too risky to hand off to anyone else?*
- *Is there someone else who could complete the task successfully?*

- *Does the task provide an opportunity for someone to develop new skills?*
- *Is there enough time to effectively delegate the task to someone?*

"Got it." Jenn said.

She was already thinking about what items on her to-do list might fit.

Tony took another sip of coffee and leaned back. *"Good. Next is **Identify the Right Individual**."*

Jenn smirked. *"You mean pick someone who won't mess it up?"*

Tony laughed. *"More like pick someone on your team who has the right mix of acquired skills and available time to handle it successfully. If you delegate to the wrong person, you're setting them up for failure."*

Jenn nodded and jotted something down. *"Okay, so I should consider their workload, and what I think they are good at."*

Tony shook his head. "But that's not all of it. Good leaders set people up for success, not struggle, when they do the next thing - **Mandate Important Metrics**."

Jenn raised an eyebrow. *"Mandate? Sounds extreme."*

Tony grinned. *"It just means being crystal clear about what success looks like. If you don't define expectations, you're asking for confusion, missed deadlines, and frustration - for both of you."*

Jenn leaned forward. *"Okay, so I need to spell out what a good job is?"*

"*Yes, good. You're not just assigning work - you're giving them a picture of what winning would look like. Define the timeline, the quality standards, and the 'why' behind the task. If they don't understand why it matters, they won't own it.*"

Jenn scribbled in her notebook. "*Got it. Clear expectations mean fewer headaches later.*"

Tony chuckled. "*Correct.*"

Jenn glanced at the last phrase. "**Extend Resources and Evaluate Progress.** *That sounds... obvious?*"

Tony smirked. "*Obvious doesn't mean easy. Think of delegation like sending someone on a road trip. You wouldn't hand them a set of keys and say, 'Good luck!' without giving them a map, gas money, or a way to call for help.*"

Jenn grinned. "*Fair point. But isn't that micromanaging? Won't they resent that?*"

"*Support isn't about looking over their shoulder, Jenn. Nobody wants that. But you should share helpful information and set up times for them to check in. Let them know you are available for any questions. And at the end, because delegation is a development opportunity, I found it helpful to ask my people 'What did you learn from this, and what would you do differently next time?'*"

Jenn leaned back in her chair, tapping her pen against her chin. "*So delegation isn't just offloading my work - it's an investment in my people.*"

Tony raised his coffee mug. "*Exactly. And your return on that investment is a stronger, more capable team - and a lot less stress for you in the long run.*"

At that exact moment, Jenn heard a deep booming voice behind her, coming from somewhere near the door. *"Well, well - if it isn't the wise old plumber himself."*

Jenn looked up to see a broad-shouldered man in his mid-forties grinning down at Tony. The man wore a dark button-down work shirt with his name, Wayne, stitched above the pocket. When he made it to their table, his hand clapped Tony on the shoulder. *"I should've known you'd be in here, changing lives one coffee at a time."*

Tony chuckled. *"Wayne! How are you doing?"*

"Just stopped in for a to-go cup of Lucia's finest before heading to the shop, but when I saw you over here, I couldn't pass up the chance to thank you... again. Business is booming, Tony. We're more profitable now, my team is happier, and I can actually enjoy my weekends."

He turned to Jenn, his smile widening. *"And I owe it all to this guy..."* Wayne pointed down at Tony, then pointed at her notebook. *"And to the stuff I wrote down in a notebook just like that. I hired him to fix the bathroom at our shop, and he ended up fixing me too."*

Jenn raised an eyebrow. *"Let me guess - you had a few coffee conversations too?"*

Wayne laughed. *"More than a few. I used to run myself ragged, getting frustrated with my team and trying to do everything myself. Tony helped me see that leadership isn't about control - it's about clarity, and trust, and..."* Wayne's eyes lit up. *"And adjusting to DO what the team needs!"*

He leaned over and tapped Jenn's notebook with his finger. *"Every lesson, every nugget, get it all down in there. And before long, you'll see things getting better. If you DO the stuff that you write down. Right, Tony?"*

Tony smiled, but his eyes twinkled with something else - maybe pride. *"Glad to hear it, Wayne."*

Wayne nodded, and looked over at the counter. *"Alright, I'll let you two get back to it."* Then to Jenn, *"You're in good hands..."* With a final grin, he left their table to head over to the register.

Jenn watched him, then turned back to Tony. *"So... you've done this a few times before?"*

Tony took a slow sip of coffee. *"Once or twice."*

Then he slid the last sheet of paper across the table. *"Now, let's talk about team meetings as that last system you can improve."*

EFFECTIVE
— L E A D E R S —

CHAPTER 10

SAFE MEETINGS

The paper Tony slid across the table to Jenn was a blank meeting agenda.

Jenn studied it. Her meetings had never been anything like this. Not even the ones she attended when she was still working as an engineer, when Susan was still the team manager. She realized that you usually lead based on the way you were led. And sometimes that was not a good thing.

Tony's voice drew her attention back to the moment. *"Team meetings are culture-building experiences, if you do them well. And they can be a waste of time if you don't. I definitely led a few that were wastes of time for my team before my aunt talked to me about what they needed to accomplish. That is what led to this template. It is a system you can use to lead better meetings with your team..."*

He pointed at the different sections on the page. *"And although this one is blank, the important parts for us today are the six things you can see there that you want to include in every meeting..."*

TEAM MEETING TEMPLATE

Date:	Time:	Place:

OUR MISSION: (why we exist)

OUR NORMS: (team standards)
1.
2.
3.
4.

TODAY'S MEETING OBJECTIVES:
1.
2.
3.

CONNECTION ACTIVITY OR QUESTION:
"What is your most memorable travel experience?"

CELEBRATION OF VALUES IN ACTION:

Person:

Reason:

MEETING AGENDA (INVITE CONTRIBUTION OF OPINIONS FOR EACH):

Time	Item (as a question)	Action Required
8:00	-	•
8:15	-	•
8:40	-	•

NEXT MEETING: DATE: TIME:

COMMITMENTS: (WHO WILL DO WHAT BY WHEN?)
•
•
•

GR GREAT RESULTS

Jenn saw more than six things on the paper she was looking at. She left the paper face up beside her notebook, and flipped a page to begin taking notes on this last system. *"So, this is kinda the summit for an effective leader?"*

Now Tony looked confused.

Jenn tried to explain. *"If systems are the top step in the evolution of leaders... you know, stuff, staff, self, systems... then this last system you are sharing would be the pinnacle, right?"*

Tony grinned. *"Well, I guess you could say that. Because it involves understanding a lot of the things we've talked about already. But I think of it more like a valuable tool that we can use to improve our self, our staff, and our stuff... if we do it right."*

He pointed to the front of her notebook. The part she had filled over the last week with so many insights and tactics. *"Remember what I said last week about the importance of interactions?"*

Jenn nodded. She did remember. It was the matrix. She didn't even have to flip back to look. *"Yeah. You said they needed to be both compelling and considerate to be productive. Why?"*

"Because if leadership is the influence of your interactions, then you need to remember that meetings are an interaction you have with your whole team. Meetings are where you equip and inspire them to be winning teammates and do their job well... and if you cancel a meeting, or treat it like it is unimportant, that in itself is an interaction."

Jenn twirled the pen in her hand, not sure if she should say anything. She didn't quite get what he was saying.

"Jenn, as a leader, everything you do is communicating something. Choosing not to send a message or have a meeting is a message in itself - you just don't have control of how people

interpret it. Sometimes silence can be deadly for a team if people make a wrong assumption about what you did. Or what you didn't do..."

"That makes sense. So, meetings are a place for me to be sure that everyone hears what they need for the team to function better together?"

"Good. Yes. And if the one-on-one meetings are a system for you to build connection and trust and develop them as individuals, team meetings have the power to accomplish even more. And because the quality of your systems usually determines the quality of your outcomes, I want to be sure you implement a process that is more likely to provide the results you are hoping to achieve..."

Jenn nodded gratefully. She was looking forward to learning more about this. She knew the meetings with her team so far had been an uninspiring collection of announcements and lukewarm engagement at best.

In large letters in the notebook, she had written that MEETINGS ARE CULTURE BUILDING EXPERIENCES. But she was unaware of how to use a weekly meeting for anything other than sharing updates and information.

Jenn noticed Wayne walking past them with a large to-go coffee in his hand. He smiled and waved a friendly goodbye to them, and Tony waved back.

Then he turned back to Jenn to continue. *"Meetings... Yes. Are you ready for the six things that you will want to include in your weekly team meetings?"*

Jenn nodded. *"Hit me."*

Tony nodded, and held up his index finger. *"Good. The first thing sounds simple, but it is important, Jenn.* **Let people know when and where the meeting is, and who should attend.** *Only invite the people who need to be there - those who have something valuable to share or who need the information that will be discussed. And give all participants plenty of notice so they can prepare and show up ready to contribute. Meeting in person is best, if you can, but you can also have effective meetings virtually if you prepare well. Let them know if you expect their cameras to be on, or if they should bring something with them. And send out a reminder the day before. People are all busy and distracted by other concerns, so be thoughtful in sharing reminders to assist them in being there on time."*

He paused and held up two fingers now. *"Which brings me to the second thing you will want to do.* **Be clear about why you're meeting and review your team mission and norms.** *If there's ever a reason you need to cancel, communicate that with your team. But every time you meet, make sure everyone knows the purpose and what's expected of each team member. Taking a moment to remind the team of their purpose and any standards of behavior you have set helps keep everyone focused and more productive..."*

"Got it. So, what's number three?" she asked.

"The third thing you want to do in every team meeting is to **add a quick activity to build connections.** *Stronger relationships lead to better teamwork and collaboration. You should invest five or ten minutes in getting everyone talking and sharing about themselves somehow. A little relationship-building goes a long way in helping develop empathy. If you have less than fifteen people in the meeting, you can just go around one at a*

time and have the group answer a fun question, like 'what is a vacation that you will never forget,' or 'what is the first concert you ever went to?'"

Tony smiled and paused, leaning back in his chair. He scratched at the gray and black stubble on his chin before continuing. *"You know, Roberto found a whole deck of these, uh, connection cards... with questions on the back. He uses them with his staff at the school... he has them get in pairs or small groups to share their answers. But, however you do it, people want to feel known, understood, and appreciated. And it doesn't take too much time to do something in a meeting to let them share something about themselves."*

Jenn was still writing when he began to jump into the next thing.

"Now, the fourth thing you want to do in every meeting is—"

"Just a sec!" Jenn demanded. She had raised her left index finger high while finishing getting the last part down on her page.

Tony chuckled at her. *"And here I thought that I wasn't ever going to go too fast for you!"*

Jenn dropped her left hand back to the table. *"Okay, ready for the fourth thing now."*

"Okay, the fourth thing is to **celebrate the behaviors you want to see more of.** *Do you recall talking about how important defining values are to your team?"*

Jenn nodded. *"Yes. The index card activity for principles."*

"Good. Well, meetings are where you get to celebrate examples of when somebody lived out the values you want others to imitate. Highlight something recent that demonstrates those values and how they affected a client or coworker or made progress toward a shared goal. Reinforcing positive behaviors builds morale and helps to clarify for the team what being a great team member looks like. You want to recognize people for doing things you want to see repeated... and reward the whole team so they all feel the benefit. Whether it's a cake, or a bonus, or something as simple as just verbal praise, help everyone feel that they get to enjoy the win."

Jenn turned the page in her notebook. *"Got it. And then there were two..."*

*"Well then. Number five is when you get to where most leaders begin. That is the nuts and bolts of the meeting, where you **walk through the agenda and invite input**. But effective leaders don't just talk at their team. They ask for input to get the team's thoughts and ideas. They make sure everyone has a chance to contribute. You want your people to feel heard and valued. Yes, ultimately there will be times when you have to make tough decisions... and meetings are where you collect the information and diverse perspectives that help you make decisions more effectively."*

Tony pointed at the paper that still sat on the table beside Jenn's notebook. *"And an easy way to make that happen is to turn the items on your agenda into a list of questions you want help answering. Too many meetings are a wasted opportunity for collecting team perspectives or suggestions. Instead..."*

He reached out and motioned with his hand, asking to use her pen. She held it out for him, smiling, and turned the notebook to face him, as she had already done a few times in the past. He wrote something and turned the notebook back to her.

On the page were the letters: **WAYSTID**.

"You want meetings to be WAYSTID opportunities! You want to go into every one of them with the intention of collecting responses to that important question - 'What Are You Seeing That I Don't?'"

"Aren't you clever!" Jenn said.

"I'm glad you like it. But it is sticky stuff like that you will remember, and what you remember you will apply and benefit from, right?"

Jenn nodded slowly. *"That makes sense, Tony... But I wonder..."* She thought a moment about someone on her team. *"What about someone like Maria?"*

Tony raised an eyebrow. *"Go on?"*

Jenn leaned back in her chair. *"Well, you know, I mentioned we had that one-on-one chat. I knew she was quiet. But I didn't realize how much she was holding in. Turns out, at her last job, the culture was brutal. Mistakes weren't just pointed at, they were punished. She told me people would get criticized in front of everyone for the tiniest errors. So, she learned to double and triple-check everything, because if she wasn't absolutely sure it was perfect, she didn't want to send it."*

Tony nodded thoughtfully. *"Perfectionism amplified by fear..."*

"Exactly," Jenn said. *"That's one reason she wasn't communicating. I think she was afraid of handing in anything*

that wasn't flawless. She figured it was better to be late than to be wrong. But that wasn't the only thing on her mind..."

Jenn sighed and looked at Tony, shaking her head. *"She also shared that her sister lost her job a few weeks ago, and since they live together, Maria's been taking on extra stress to help cover the bills. She didn't come out and say it, but I could tell she's exhausted. Between the pressure she puts on herself at work and the stress at home, she's completely drained."*

Tony leaned back. *"That's a lot to carry."*

Jenn nodded. *"It really is. So I told her that mistakes aren't the end of the world. And that it was important to let people know what was going on, and not wait to turn something in."*

Tony smiled. *"Good..."*

"Yeah, I think she felt relieved. But I also think she's someone who will be uncomfortable sharing stuff in meetings with the group, even if I ask, you know?"

Tony picked up his coffee. *"You're learning fast, Jenn."*

"What do you mean?"

"I mean, your awareness. Seeing her behavior as a symptom of the real issue. And understanding that YOU need to adjust to help her succeed..."

Jenn grinned, and let out an amused snort through her nose. *"Watch out. I'll be turning into a wrench if you're not careful."*

"What you are noticing that Maria needs is actually important for everyone, Jenn. It's called psychological safety. And it is the feeling that people get that it is okay to share an

idea, admit a mistake, or ask a question. Without getting punished for it..."

Tony pointed at her notebook. *"Write this down. It will help you get more participation during the agenda part of your meetings. Psychological safety is what allows teams to communicate openly, learn from mistakes, and grow together..."*

"So how is it different from trust, then?" she asked.

"Well, trust is about making one person feel safe. Psychological safety is about making sure everyone on the team does. It helps when you ask open-ended questions on the agenda - and when you encourage people to share different ideas and healthy disagreement. I would even designate someone as a 'negative Ned', who was responsible for challenging ideas and bringing up problems. You want them to get comfortable with putting their truth on the table..."

He patted the table with his hand for emphasis. *"And something else I did early on to help build that safety was ending our meetings by inviting participants to send me an email afterwards and reply to this simple question - 'What needed to be said today that wasn't?' That gave the team permission to shine a light on issues they felt deserved more attention."*

"Did people really send you emails about it?"

"Well, the key is follow-through..." Tony said, leaning forward again. *"When you get responses, you need to acknowledge and thank them for every comment and mention them during your next meeting if you want to reinforce that sharing their perspective is valued. You don't want people to leave the meeting and have conversations or share texts they weren't willing to*

bring up with you. What they think needs to be said should be brought out of the shadows."

"Okay..." Jenn said, as she wrote. *"And number six?"*

*"That is the last part of every meeting. **Wrap up with commitments and next steps.** That is where you confirm who's going to do what and by when. And then follow up with a quick email summary to recap the discussion points from the meeting and the actions that people promised to take... then you remind everyone when the next meeting is!"*

Jenn looked at her watch as she finished writing the last point. She was already thinking about getting back home to take Dooley to his grooming appointment, before she had a couple of virtual calls.

The Bakersfield project was close to going into production. And she wanted to be sure to have good news to share with Lewis when they talked next week. *"Is that it for today, then?"*

"That is the last system for now, Jenn. And the last part of the evolution of focus lesson that I promised..."

Jenn scrunched up her face, looking down at all she had written today. And then considered the many full pages of notes she had taken during their coffee conversations. *"You said when we started that you'd share four lessons, Tony. But, I gotta say, it's getting a little jumbled up in my head with all the parts and steps and..."* She shook her head, discouraged by her inability to organize it all in her head.

Tony just smiled... *"We have certainly covered a lot, Jenn. Reviewing it will help. Want to do that now?"*

Jenn frowned at herself for needing to, but nodded. *"Let me try..."* she said, and flipped to the front of the now flimsy spiral notebook filled with her handwriting.

"First we talked about the Ladder of Awareness..." She talked as she turned the pages. *"And moving past symptoms to problems and solutions... and then the Cycle of Culture and how awareness affects behaviors and experiences... and that leadership is the influence of interactions, and..."*

She paused as she flipped and skimmed over the pages. "The *Interaction Matrix for productive conversations.... All that was about Awareness. And then the second lesson... that was about assumptions."*

"Good so far," Tony encouraged her.

Jenn didn't look up. She was determined to get everything they had discussed so far more logically ordered in her head. *"And the lesson on assumptions was about examining the stories we tell ourselves. About our purpose... and principles... and people... and politeness."*

With a quiet rustle, she turned another page, and her index finger traced a quick path down the lines of information she had collected.

Tony watched her processing, and did not interrupt.

"And the third lesson..." Jenn continued, her finger finding the third set of four steps she had drawn, *"was the one we just finished. The Evolution of Focus. From stuff... to improving my staff with one-on-one conversations and feedback... to asking better questions and developing myself..."*

Jenn flipped more quickly now through the last few pages. They were fresh on her mind. *"And then the top of that was moving from focusing on myself to focusing on systems... the starting five, delegation, and better meetings."*

Tony's eyes were wide above his grin as he responded. *"I'm proud of you, Jenn. That is a good summary. Sounds like you've got a better handle on it than you thought?"*

She nodded, and began to close her notebook.

"Let me offer this, though, before you put the notebook away. Meetings really are culture building opportunities. And each one we've talked about needs to have a place on your calendar. The one-on-one conversations for weekly interactions with individuals, the weekly team meetings for keeping everyone aligned and collecting their ideas, and then the quarterly events for focusing on strategy or team building..."

Jenn jotted that down dutifully, and then closed the notebook flat, sliding the meeting template inside it before standing up. *"Tony, I really am grateful for this..."*

"Guess I'll see you on Friday, then, for our last lesson?" he asked.

"Confidence, right?"

"Good. Yes. And keep reviewing your notes. That will help..."

"Oh, yes. Definitely." Jenn replied.

"Now, I'm off for an errand, and then I've got a few interactions to prepare for later today. I'll see you Friday morning!"

EFFECTIVE
— LEADERS —

CHAPTER 11

HELPING OTHERS

On Thursday evening at around 10:15 pm, Jenn heard someone outside.

She was sitting on the couch, Dooley in her lap looking adorable from his grooming earlier that week, watching an old 20/20 episode she had recorded when there was a noise on the front porch. This was her last night alone, and she was already on edge.

She stood up with Dooley under one arm and peeked around the corner at the front door entryway. And she could see the knob turning!

A moment later, the door swung open, and her husband was standing in front of her. Brian swept her up in a tight hug. *"Surprise!"* he grinned, dropping his bags.

Jenn hit him playfully on the shoulder. *"You scared me to death!"*

"I changed my ticket to get on the last flight home today. Gotta help the team unload when they return to campus tomorrow. Thought you'd be happy about it!"

She laughed, hugging him back. *"You have no idea how good it is to see you."*

The next morning, they enjoyed coffee together for the first time in over two weeks. She was so excited to have him home. Then she glanced at her phone. It was nearly 7:30 am.

She needed to text Tony and cancel their meeting. With Brian home early, she wanted to soak in every moment she could.

Her thumbs worked the screen.

"Hey Tony, Brian just got back.

I'm going to take the morning off.

Can we reschedule for next week sometime?"

Tony's reply came within seconds.

"Of course. Thursday would be best.

Same time and place. Enjoy!"

She didn't get much of anything done for work the rest of that morning. Luckily, there were no meetings on her schedule that day. But after lunch, Brian was getting ready to leave again.

He had to meet the team back at campus to help the other coaches unload the uniforms and equipment and ensure everything was back in its place and ready for the upcoming season, following their team trip overseas.

She rubbed her temples a few minutes later as he left. It had been a whirlwind couple of weeks. And with that thought, she grabbed her notebook, flipped through the pages, and found herself staring at the last few blank sheets in the back.

Only six pages left. That was for the final lesson - Confidence.

She leaned back against the couch. Her notes were overflowing with insights and reflections from conversations that had reshaped the way she saw leadership.

There was so much to process. She would definitely need to go over it all again - probably multiple times - to fully absorb everything Tony had shared with her.

One truth had settled in her chest with certainty, though. Her purpose as a leader wasn't about control or proving herself. It was about serving, supporting, caring for, and developing others. She bit her pen as she looked over the pages.

And she thought about Maria and Dan.

She grabbed her phone and pulled up the Google Maps app. First, she selected a restaurant near where Maria lived. Then she found another near Dan's home address.

A few minutes later, she sent Maria a text message.

"Hey Maria - Just wanted to take a moment to admit it was a challenge for me to adjust to this role, and I appreciate your patience and support. Dinner with your sister is on me. Check your email for a gift card. I hope you both take a break and enjoy a meal out together. I'm really glad to have you on the team!"

She hit send and smiled. It wasn't much, but hopefully they would enjoy it.

Then she sent a similar message to Dan, so he knew she was thinking of him, and so he and his wife could enjoy a dinner together.

Her phone buzzed a few moments later.

But it wasn't Maria or Dan. It was a message from Tony. *"Jenn. I've been thinking about our last conversation regarding meetings. And I wanted to add that team communication doesn't always need to be in person. It just needs to be helpful and thoughtful. If you clarify with team members* when it's okay to reach out, so you don't disrupt their protected time for deep work, or for their family, you will find that those interactions can be very valuable.

"Some of the best comments or insights can happen when people have space to reflect before responding. My team has found that online platforms can be a terrific place to upload, edit, and comment on topics that others can then benefit from.

"Of course, it doesn't diminish the power and impact of in-person meetings, but it can certainly augment your team productivity. Some of the most helpful collaboration on teams can take place outside of live meetings. Like this text I'm sending you!"

Jenn read the long text twice, nodding. That was a good reminder. Meetings were important, but so was respecting people's time and preferences. Not every discussion needed to be in a conference room.

A moment later, she got another text from him.

"Also, I'm confident you'll benefit from our lesson Thursday morning.

See you then!"

The last message made her chuckle.

She flipped through the notebook again, reading assorted pages quietly to herself as she waited on Brian to return home...

———

By the time Tuesday morning had arrived, she and Brian had returned to their same comfortable cadence of meals, watching shows, and being home together. But he did say on two different occasions that she seemed "different." And he was very deliberate to explain that he meant it in a good way. Like she was more comfortable with her job now.

She was glad for the time they had spent apart. Much more glad, really, than she ever expected to be - because now she was equipped with the insights and tactics to do her job better.

Now she just needed to convince Lewis of that. And they had a meeting scheduled for later this morning, now that he was back from his vacation and ready to refocus on her performance.

Brian was already gone to the gym for workouts and skill sessions with a few of the players, and Jenn was getting herself ready to go into the office. Tuesday was her in-person day.

Part of her was excited to try out the new meeting agenda she had been working on. She had sent it out to the team yesterday after lunch. But part of her couldn't help but feel anxious - would the template actually shift the team's indifferent mood or make a real difference in their culture?

Jenn was mid-sip of her second coffee when her phone rang. It was Lewis. She set down her mug and answered. *"Good morning, Lewis."*

"Morning, Jenn. How's the first of September treating you?"

"So far, so good. You?"

"Can't complain. The beach was nice." His voice was warm, but direct. *"Listen, I wanted to check in, but I'm not gonna make it to the office today for our meeting. So, any updates on how things are going?"*

Jenn leaned back, and took a breath. *"Actually, yes. I've been making some adjustments, getting more comfortable in the role. It's been a good two weeks. I feel like we're making progress."*

"Glad to hear that." There was a pause, then a light chuckle. *"You know, I've been hearing good things. A few people I've spoken to say they think you're settling in."*

Jenn blinked. *"Really?"*

"Really. They say you're communicating more. That's good. Leadership isn't about getting everything perfect - it's about growing into the role." There was a beat of silence. *"You know, adjusting..."*

She smiled, taking that in.

"Speaking of adjusting," Lewis continued, *"I want you to know that there will always be storms. Unexpected obstacles, tough moments, messy situations. But those storms? They're opportunities. Opportunities to connect more. To recommit. To grow."*

Jenn's reached for her notebook and a pen. She wanted to be sure to get his words down. That comment sounded like something Tony would say...

"Anyway, be grateful for problems," Lewis continued. *"They force us to evolve. But the question is - what's the story you want your team to tell after the storm has passed? Will they remember you as a leader who panicked, or one who adjusted? Will your example inspire them to see problems as frustrations, or as invitations to grow?"*

Jenn exhaled, letting those words sink in.

"Good leaders adjust," Lewis added, his voice steady. *"And with the right mentor or coach, they become exactly what their team needs."*

She nodded, even though he couldn't see her. *"Thanks, Lewis. I needed that."*

"We all do," he said. *"Keep going, Jenn. You're gonna be just fine."*

As the call ended, Jenn looked down at her newest few lines of notes. Then she peered out the window to check the weather. The sky was clear this morning.

Of course, she knew that storms would come. They always did. But today, she felt more ready for them.

CHAPTER 12

GROWING CONFIDENCE

Thursday morning arrived with a crispness that hinted at the coming autumn. It was the kind of morning that begged for a steaming cup of coffee, and Jenn was more than happy to oblige. When she arrived at the coffee shop, Tony was already there, sipping from a large to-go cup instead of his usual ceramic mug.

"Busy morning?" she asked, sliding into the seat across from him.

"Yep," Tony nodded. *"Got a new guy starting today. Not a leak this time, thank goodness. Just need to help him get up to speed. Investing in a new teammate is just as important as fixing pipes. Maybe more."*

Tony pointed his thumb back at the counter. *"You might want to grab a to-go coffee too, this is probably the shortest lesson of all."*

Tony leaned back in his chair. *"Because confidence is less about knowing, and more about doing. It's what you do after today that will determine the value of what I'm gonna say..."*

Jenn raised an eyebrow, and then hurried to the counter to get the dark roast she had been looking forward to on the familiar ride over to Deja-Brew. When she returned, she placed the large to-go coffee on the table and took the spiral notebook and a pen out of her purse. *"Okay. I'm caffeinated and curious!"*

Tony took a thoughtful sip of his coffee, then smiled. *"You know, when I talk about confidence, I like telling the story of my son Roberto when we took him to the beach one summer. I mean, at first, he was scared to go out in the water past his ankles. But little by little, he went further, got comfortable, and even started swimming. And before we knew it, he was thirty feet from the shore, diving down and coming up with a handful of little baby sand dollars. They became his most treasured souvenirs from our whole trip to Florida."*

Jenn tilted her head and grinned at him. *"So, confidence is... like sand dollars?"*

Tony grinned. *"No... Confidence is the souvenir of past success that inspires positive expectations. Confidence is a belief. But it has to be based on evidence. Think about it this way... You can read about swimming, talk about it, think about it, but it's impossible to grow confident in your ability to swim if you stay dry."*

Jenn nodded, absorbing the metaphor. *"So, it requires taking action."*

"Good, yes." Tony said. *"Teams don't change because of what*

leaders think. They change because of how leaders act. All confidence comes from action."

He leaned forward. *"Without confidence, even the good strategies can fail. Confidence fuels belief, initiative, and perseverance. It turns obstacles into opportunities. And it is nothing more than you believing in your ability to navigate a challenge and figure things out."*

"Even when it's not perfect?" Jenn's mind understandably went to Maria.

Tony pointed at her notebook. *"Write this down. Four steps to confidence... And then draw your four steps, like we did with the other three lessons that we covered."*

He waited until her pen was ready again, then held up a single finger. *"First, on the bottom step, is **Courage.** Any confidence you want is on the other side of discomfort. You can't build confidence without facing something that makes you uneasy. Acknowledge that reality and be willing to welcome that conflict. Whether it's a difficult conversation, a skill you don't have yet, or a situation that feels bigger than you, step into it. Avoiding it won't make it disappear. It just makes it harder to deal with later."*

Tony raised a second finger. *"Second step. **Clarity.** You have to get clear on the skills you need to enjoy the success you want. A plumber shows up to a job and has to figure out what tools are needed to do the job. And if he doesn't have the right tools, he needs to get them if he wants to get paid. Same with leadership. Same with anything. You've gotta identify the learning and abilities required."*

He made an okay sign with his hand now. Three fingers up. *"The third step is **Cultivation**. This is the part most people don't like. Confidence comes from experience, but experience starts with struggle. Nobody walks into a new role, a new skill, or a tough situation, and nails it perfectly the first time. The people with the most confidence? They're the ones who kept trying when they felt awkward or got frustrated. They were willing to practice and be bad long enough to get better."*

Finally, he held up all four fingers. *"And last, at the top, is **Competence**. Confidence is about knowing you have done something well before, so you believe you can do it again. And competence comes from repetition, and proving to yourself that you can do something well even in adversity. That is the last step in building confidence."*

He put his hand down and looked at Jenn. *"Pretty easy, huh?"*

Jenn was done writing, but was still thinking about what he had said. *"Guess it's easier to hear than to do?"*

Tony held up his coffee to cheer her understanding. *"You don't get confidence. You earn it. You earn it by following these four steps over and over again. You give yourself permission to learn and get better as you work to develop your awareness, challenge your assumptions, and refine your focus. Because effective leaders don't wait until they have all the answers,"* he said. *"They step in, take action, and learn as they go."*

Jenn read the four steps again, letting the lesson settle in her mind. *"And if they don't?"*

Tony gave a half-smile. *"Then they become defective leaders, people who complain about the lack of results that their own lack of action created."*

Jenn exhaled, shaking her head. *"So, kinda progress over the paralysis of perfection?"*

"Now you're getting it," Tony said, pushing back his chair. *"Alright, kid. Time for me to help my new guy. You've got work to do, too."*

Jenn smiled, knowing he was right. *"Yes, I do,"* she said. *"Oh, and by the way, the game Brian got you tickets for will be the night of October 22nd. There will be six tickets waiting at will-call. And I'll be sure to meet you all there at your seats before the game starts."*

Tony gave her a thumbs up and headed out the door.

———

The stadium buzzed with energy as fans poured in, their cheers mixing with the aroma of popcorn and hotdogs. Jenn was on the home side, standing in the concourse amid the bustle of fans and concessions. She walked over to look into the arena, scanning the crowd.

Then, she saw them - Tony was there with his whole family. His grandson Nicolas bouncing excitedly next to him. Tony's daughter, Lucia, was there with her husband. And Roberto was with them too.

Jenn walked down and greeted them. She warmly thanked each of them for their generous part in helping her grow as a leader. Then, she turned to Nicolas and handed him a small gift bag. *"I knew your granddad wouldn't accept a gift,"* she said with a wink, *"but I wanted to do something to show how much I appreciate your whole family."*

Nicolas tore into the gift bag, pulling out a brand-new team jersey with his name stitched across the back, the number 1 beneath it. His face lit up as he bounced on his toes, hugging the jersey to his chest.

Not to be outdone, Tony responded by telling Jenn he had something for her as well. He handed her a white gift-wrapped box. It was nearly a foot long, but not very deep or wide. It looked like it could be jewelry, but when Jenn opened it, she laughed out loud.

An adjustable wrench.

"Something to remember me by," Tony said, grinning.

Jenn was still laughing when she noticed an empty seat in their row. Brian had reserved them six tickets. Just as she was about to ask if the last seat was going to be used, she spotted someone making their way down the steps. It was her boss, Lewis, carrying a tray filled with snacks and candy.

When Lewis continued all the way down the steps and joined Tony's family, handing out food to each of them, Jenn could only blink in surprise. Lewis just chuckled at her expression. *"Tony and I grew up near each other,"* he explained. *"He was a few years older than me. We played together as kids. His Aunt Lena helped both of us when we got started in business. And Tony's always been much better at teaching than I am. So, when I found out you had a plumbing problem that morning, I saw a perfect opportunity..."*

Jenn thought back to her last conversation with Lewis. He had mentioned adjusting a few times, hadn't he? Now, it all made sense.

———

The game was a blowout. Brian's team won big against an outmatched opponent.

"Early-season games like this," he had told her, *"are scheduled wins. A chance to build confidence."*

As they walked to the car, though, Brian surprised her by complaining. He grumbled about issues with a few of their players. Jenn slid into the passenger seat and pulled the wrench from her bag, holding it up with a playful smirk. *"Guess I'm gonna have to show you how to use this."*

Brian gave her a confused look.

She smiled. *"Have I told you about what I learned these past few weeks?"*

As he backed out of the parking space, Jenn started talking. She talked about awareness, assumptions, focus, and confidence... the lessons Tony had talked about with her over coffees.

And as she spoke, she realized just how much she had changed.

She was excited about doing **What Effective Leaders DO**.

WANT TO DOWNLOAD ALL OF
TONY'S PRINTABLE ILLUSTRATIONS
FROM THE STORY?

Grab a Copy of Jenn's Notebook of Visual Reminders–

And Instant Access to 50 Other Leadership Resources

AT WWW.TOOLBOXSTUFF.COM

ABOUT THE AUTHOR

Sean Glaze is an author and leadership speaker who has worked with clients like the CDC, John Deere, Coca-Cola, and Emory University to increase collaboration, boost productivity, and build exceptional workplace cultures. Sean's engaging conference keynotes and interactive team building events help effective leaders build Sticky Cultures.

As a successful basketball coach and educator for over 20 years, Sean gained valuable insights into leading winning teams - and founded **Effective Leaders** and **Great Results Teambuilding** to share those lessons and help organizations improve their team performance!

Find him on the following Social Media platforms

facebook.com/GreatResultsTeambuilding

x.com/leadyourteam

youtube.com/SeanGlaze

linkedin.com/in/seanglaze

amazon.com/Sean-Glaze/e/B00E6GSCEA

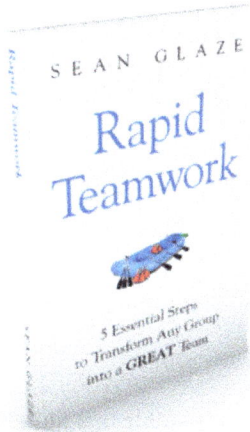

SEAN GLAZE

Rapid
Teamwork

5 Essential Steps
to Transform Any Group
into a **GREAT** Team

Rapid Teamwork tells the story of Greg Sharpe, a manager that readers can easily relate to. Greg's team has been underachieving and struggling with a few issues – but as a leader, he is unsure how to transform his group into a cohesive team.

What he and his executive team experience during an unusual rafting retreat is a series of lessons on how to become a more productive team quickly – creating a stronger, more unified workforce.

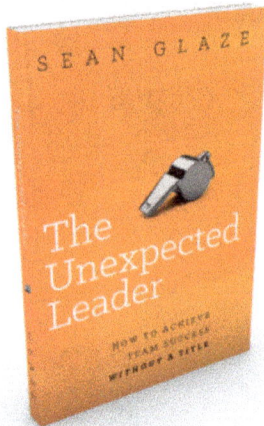

The Unexpected Leader is a parable that illustrates the importance of leading from where you are, regardless of title. It follows Matthew, a high school athlete, as he learns the power of vision, the impact of his words, and the influence that one person can have on their team.

This is a story that shares five steps that will inspire individuals to step up and lead during difficulty or change with intention and enthusiasm.

The 10 Commandments of Winning Teammates is the story of Nick Turner, a talented employee who finds himself changing jobs – again.

As he travels to his new job, he has a series of interesting interactions that illustrate the importance of the 10 commandments his coach had emphasized years earlier. The ten lessons that Nick benefits from during his journey to his next job will inspire you to be a winning teammate – regardless of the industry you work in.

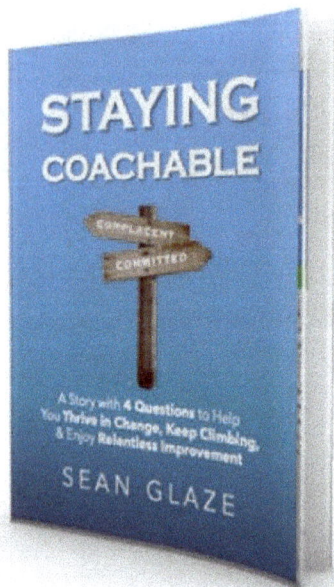

Staying Coachable tells the story of Wallace and Max Cooper, a father and son who are both experiencing the challenges of change.

What they learn from an unlikely mentor about a commitment to climbing will empower and equip you for relentless growth! This is a story that shares four questions that will inspire individuals to step up and lead during difficulty or change with intention and enthusiasm.

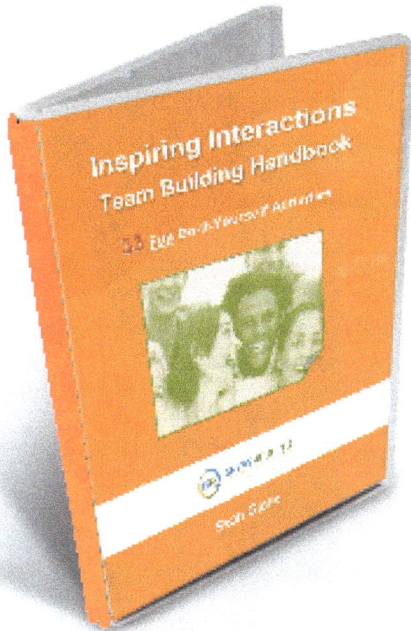

<u>Inspiring Interactions team building handbook</u> is a DIY guide for leaders who want specific activities and instructions to engage their team.

If you want to organize and facilitate your own team building challenges and discussion at your next meeting, or if you simply want to maintain the momentum that a fun team building program or keynote has created, grab your own collection of memorable interactive ideas and instructions!

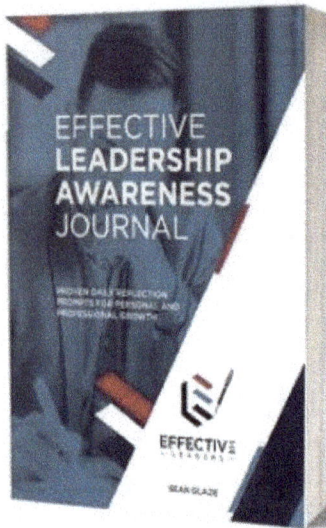

Effective Leadership Awareness Journal provides you with daily reflection prompts and activities to grow yourself so that you have more positive impact on your team.

Becoming more effective as a leader requires continuous growth, self- awareness, and the ability to adapt and respond to new challenges – and one of the most powerful tools that can significantly accelerate leadership growth and development is the practice of reflection.

All Sean's books are on his Amazon Author Page

https://bit.ly/sean-glaze

CONTACT SEAN!

Book Sean as a Speaker to **Equip Your People to Lead and Work Together More Effectively** at Your Next Corporate Event or Conference

Visit Him Online at:
https://stickycultures.com

sticky cultures

or
https://greatresultsteambuilding.com

www.ingramcontent.com/pod-product-compliance
Lightning Source LLC
Chambersburg PA
CBHW050238270326
41914CB00041BA/2034/J